AF727050

WINDOWS TO DREAM WORLDS
THE ART AND ILLUSTRATION OF JOHN LAWRY

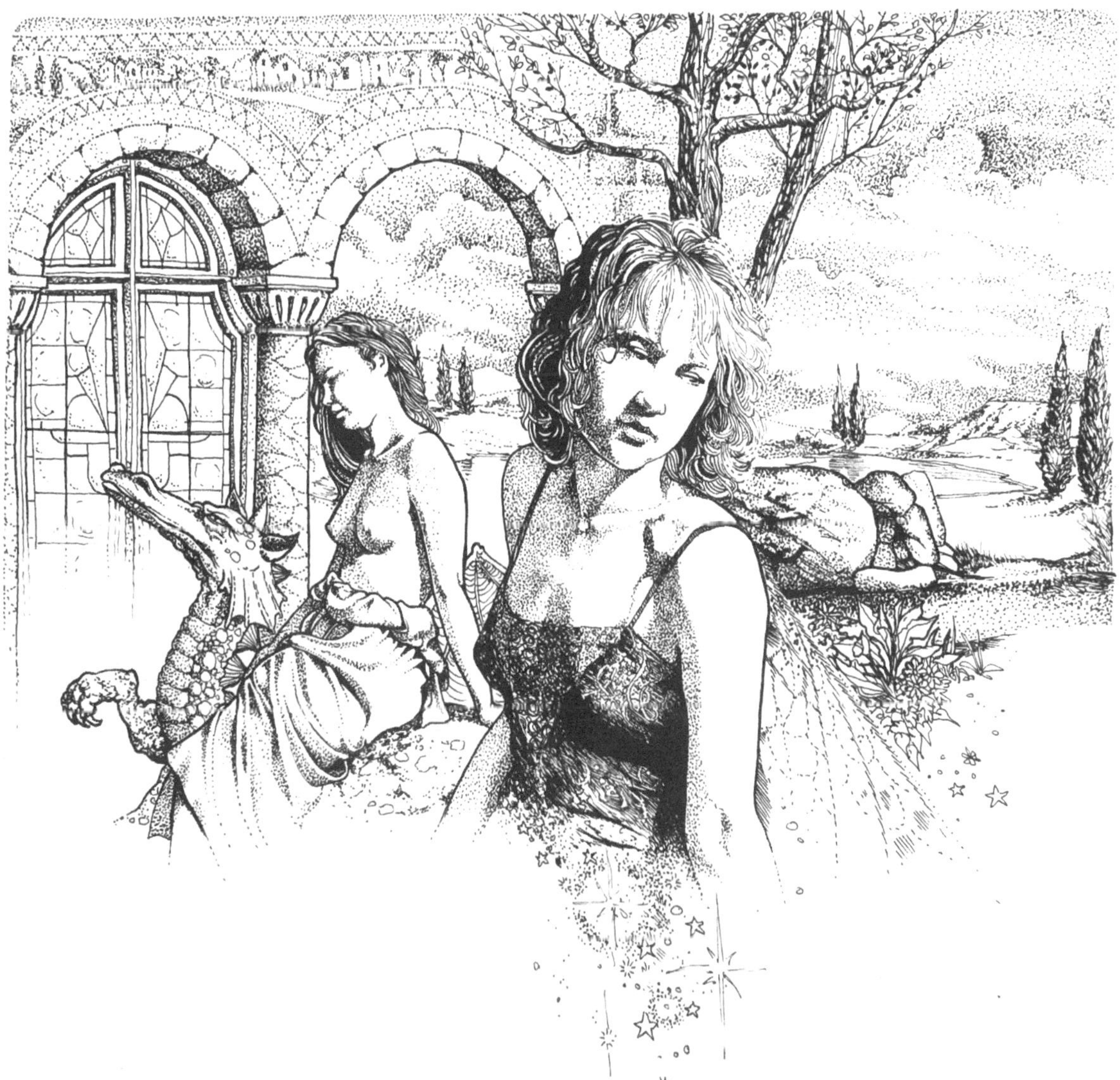

ISBN-13: 978-0-6481710-5-8

CONTENTS

5 *Cougar*, watercolour on paper, Graphic Novel – Hecate 2019
6 *Hecate*, watercolour on paper, Graphic Novel – Hecate 2019
7 *Shine and the Wizard*, oil on canvas, poster – 2017
8 *Future City*, oil on paper, poster – 2016
9 *Home of the Tree*, watercolour and oil on paper, first edition – Moon Rise 2017
10 *Arbor*, watercolour on paper, Legion 1 2018
11 *Shine and Dale*, oil on paper, back cover – Moon Shadow 2018
12 *Michelle and Sun*, watercolour on paper, Sun on the Forest 2018
13 *Future City 2,* watercolour on paper, Number 8 – Legion 1 2018
14 *Shine*, gouache on paper, front cover (detail) – Moon Shadow 2018
15 *Sun*, watercolour on paper, front cover (detail) – Sun on the Forest 2018
16 *Shine of the Moon*, watercolour on paper, front cover (detail) – Abnegation 2019
17 *The Dunwich Boys*, ink and watercolour on paper, cover – story by Eddie Hedington 2018
18 *Meadow's house*, watercolour on paper, Catcher's Keeper by Shelley Hall 2015
19 *Catcher*, watercolour on paper, Catcher's Keeper by Shelley Hall 2015
20 *Earth*, watercolour on board, City of Waverley Collection, 1988
21 *Crystal Ball*, watercolour on board, Paper Bow Tie Cards 1992
22 *Tea Party*, watercolour on board, Hallmark Calendar 2000
23 *Mermaid*, watercolour on board, Paper Bow Tie Cards 1992
24 *Sugar Plum Tree*, watercolour on board, Short story by Tony Barber 1995
25 *Sugar Plum Fairy*, watercolour on board, Short story by Tony Barber 1995
26 *Seaside*, watercolour on board, Hallmark Calendar 2000
27 *There's a Dragon Outside*, watercolour on board, unpublished book 1995
28 *Arabian Nights*, watercolour on board, Paper Bow Tie Cards 1992
29 *Magical Faerie Caravan*, watercolour on board, unpublished book 1995
30 *Christmas Shepherd*, watercolour on paper, self published cards 1998
31 *Vortex*, oil on canvas 2007
32 *Pinnacle,* oil on canvas 2008
33 *Balanced Wisdom*, oil on canvas 2008
34 *Tuscan Dream*, oil on canvas 2006
35 *Unicorn*, oil on canvas 2009
36 *Starfish*, oil on canvas 2008
37 *Guardian Spirit*, oil on canvas 2010
38 *Reevit*, oil on canvas, front cover – Legion 1 2019
39 *Float*, oil on board 2010
40 *Guardian Angel*, oil on canvas 2011
41 *Shelley in the City*, watercolour and oil on paper, poster 2018
42 *Stop*, ink and charcoal on paper, poster 2005
43 *Non-conformist*, watercolour on paper, Catcher's Keeper by Shelley Hall 2015
44 *Future World,* acrylic on canvas, back cover – Legion I 2019
45 *Green Studio*, acrylic on canvas 2010
46 *Later that Night*, Oil on Canvas 2010
47 *Link,* acrylic on canvas 2010
48 *Angel Over St Kilda*, watercolour on paper, poster 2002
49 *Lost at Southgate*, watercolour on paper, poster 2002
50 *Nightmare*, Oil on Canvas 2010
51 *Forest Creature*, ink on paper, detail from Moon Rise 2017

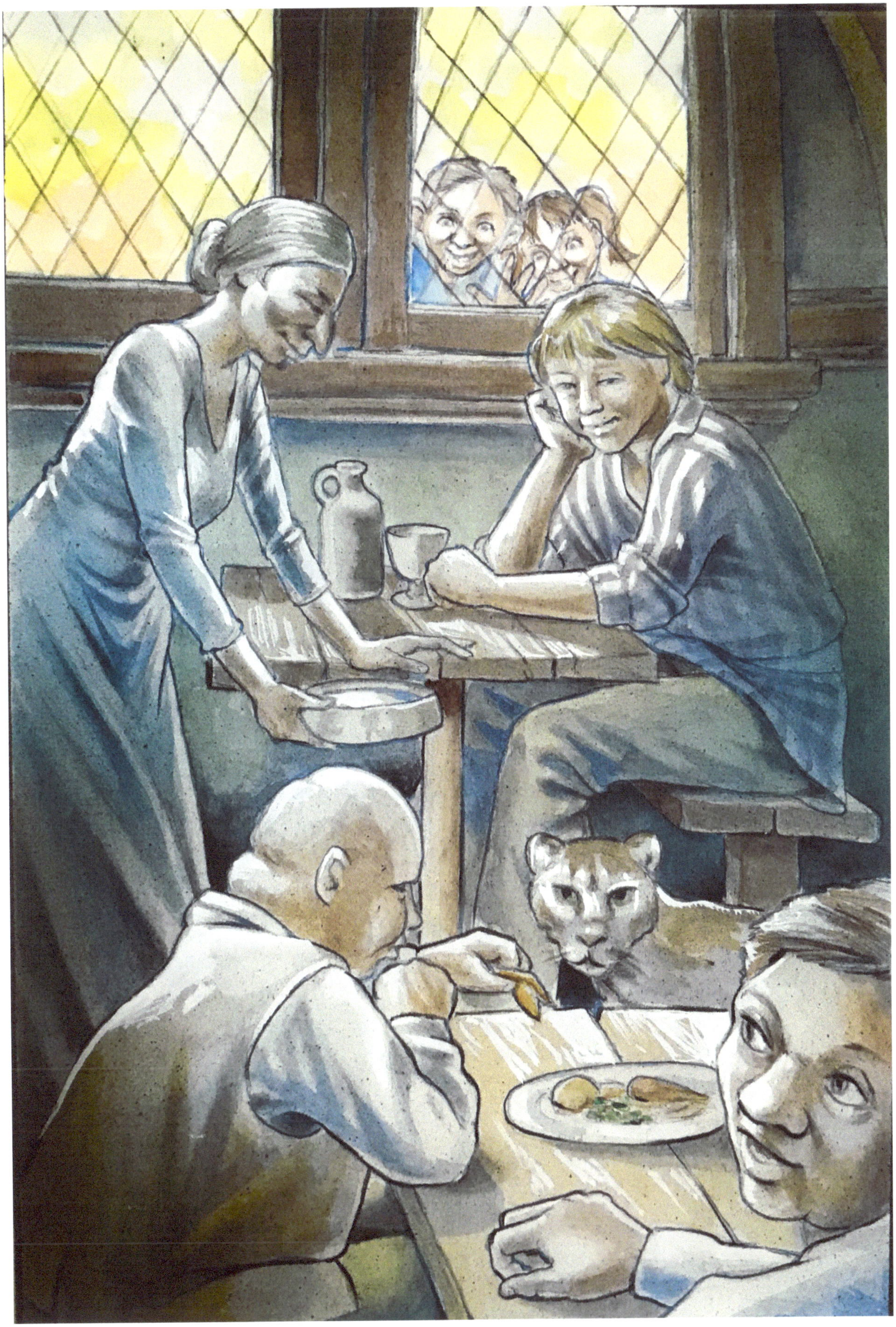

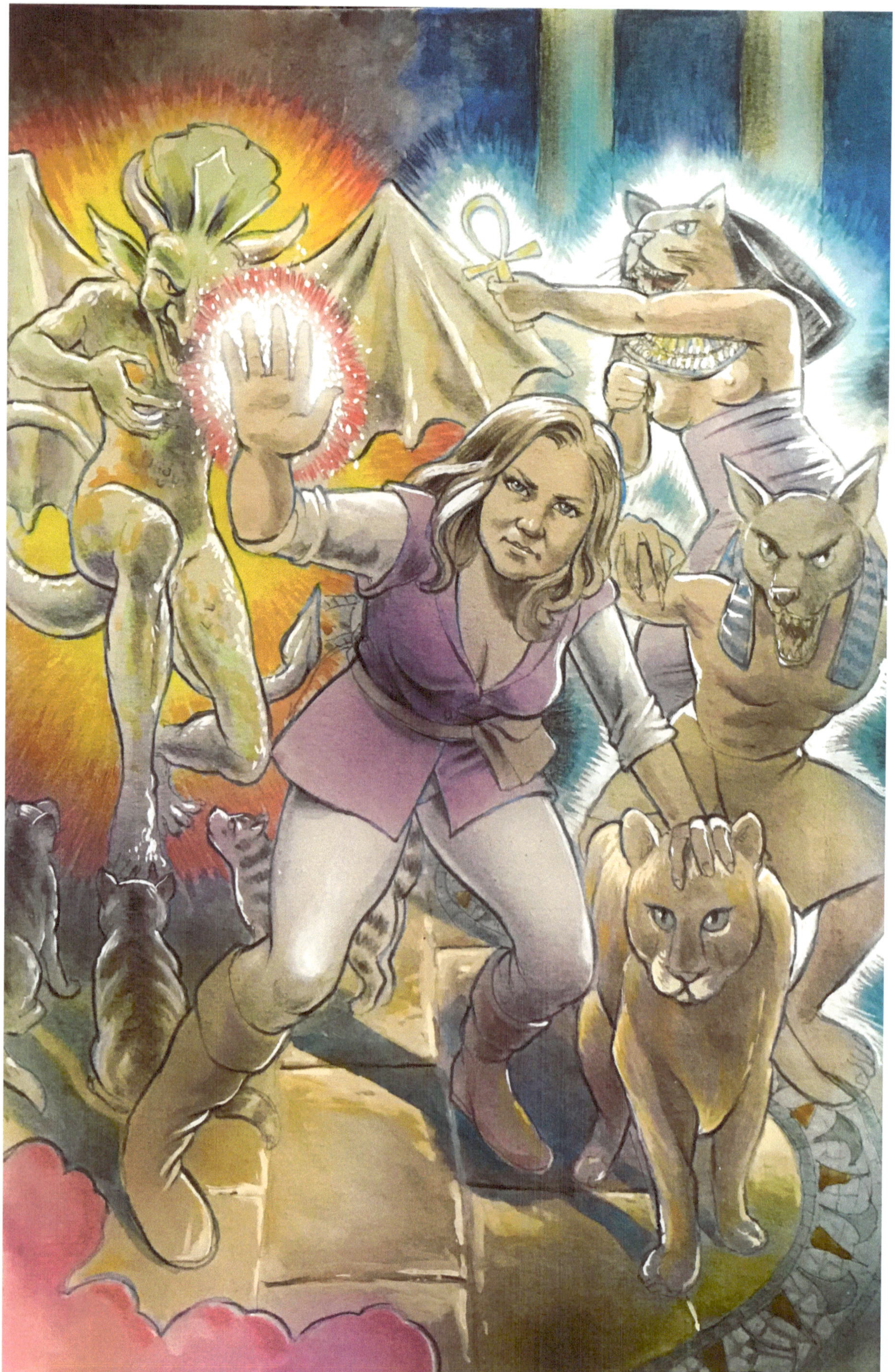

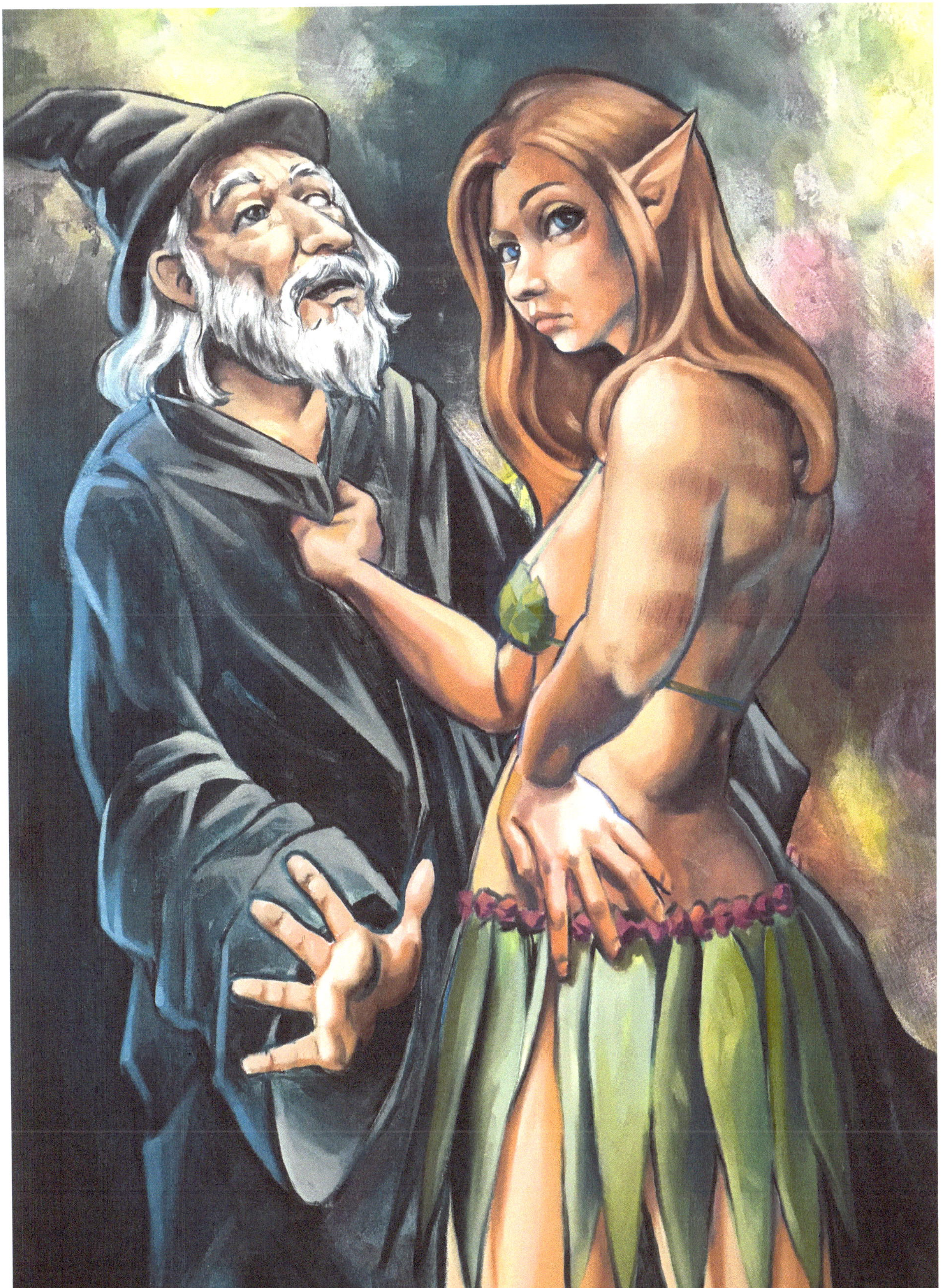

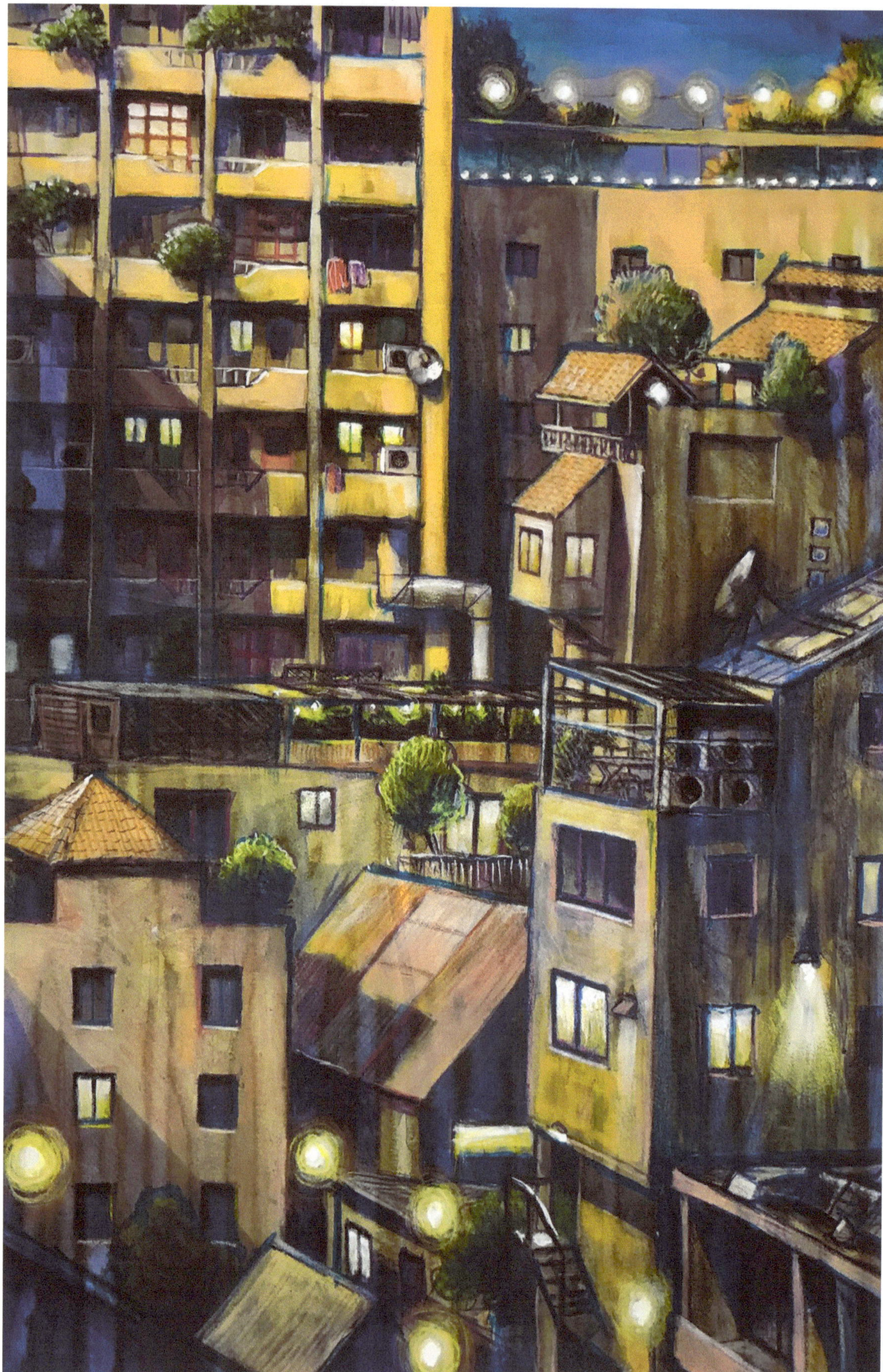

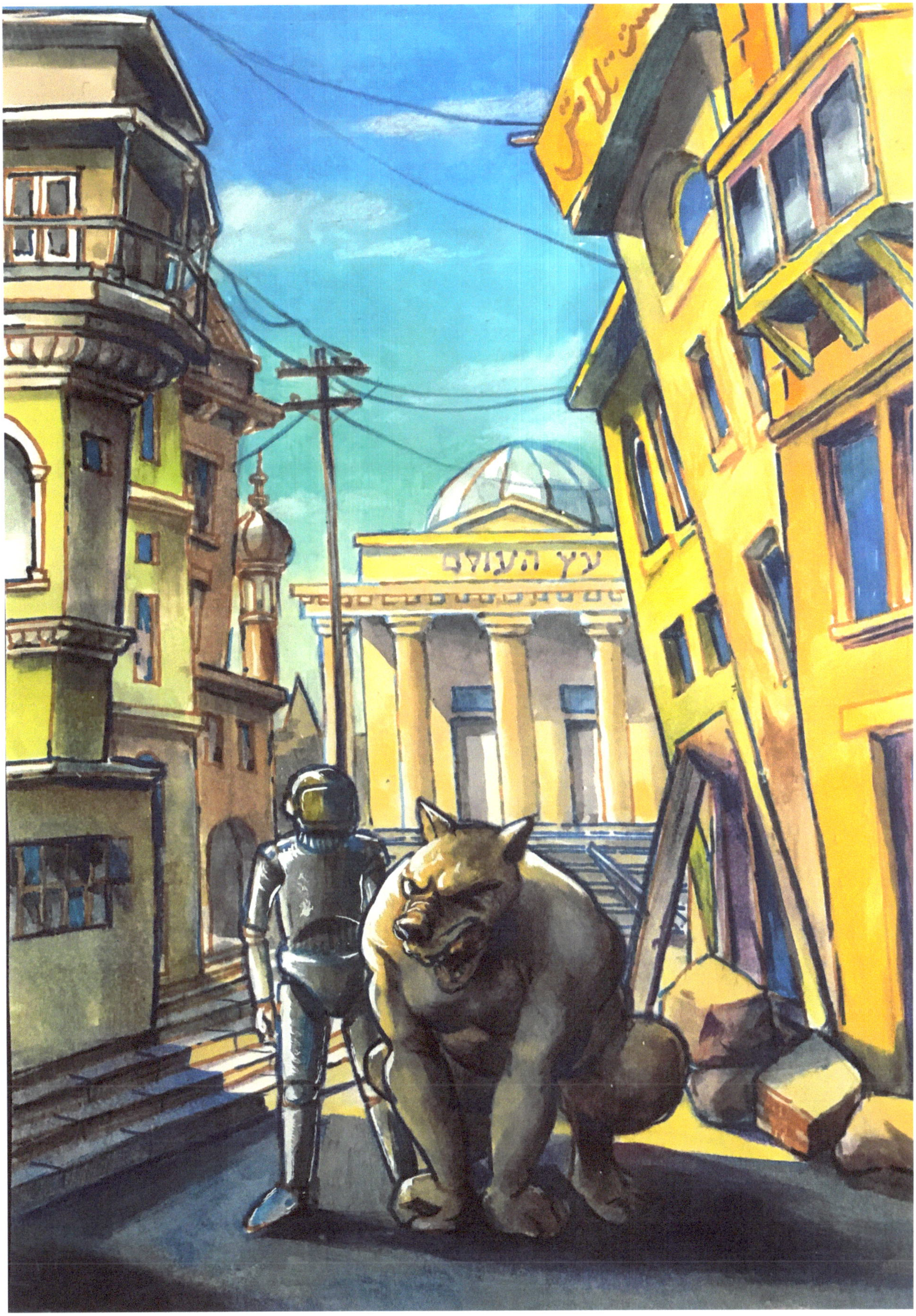
עץ העולם

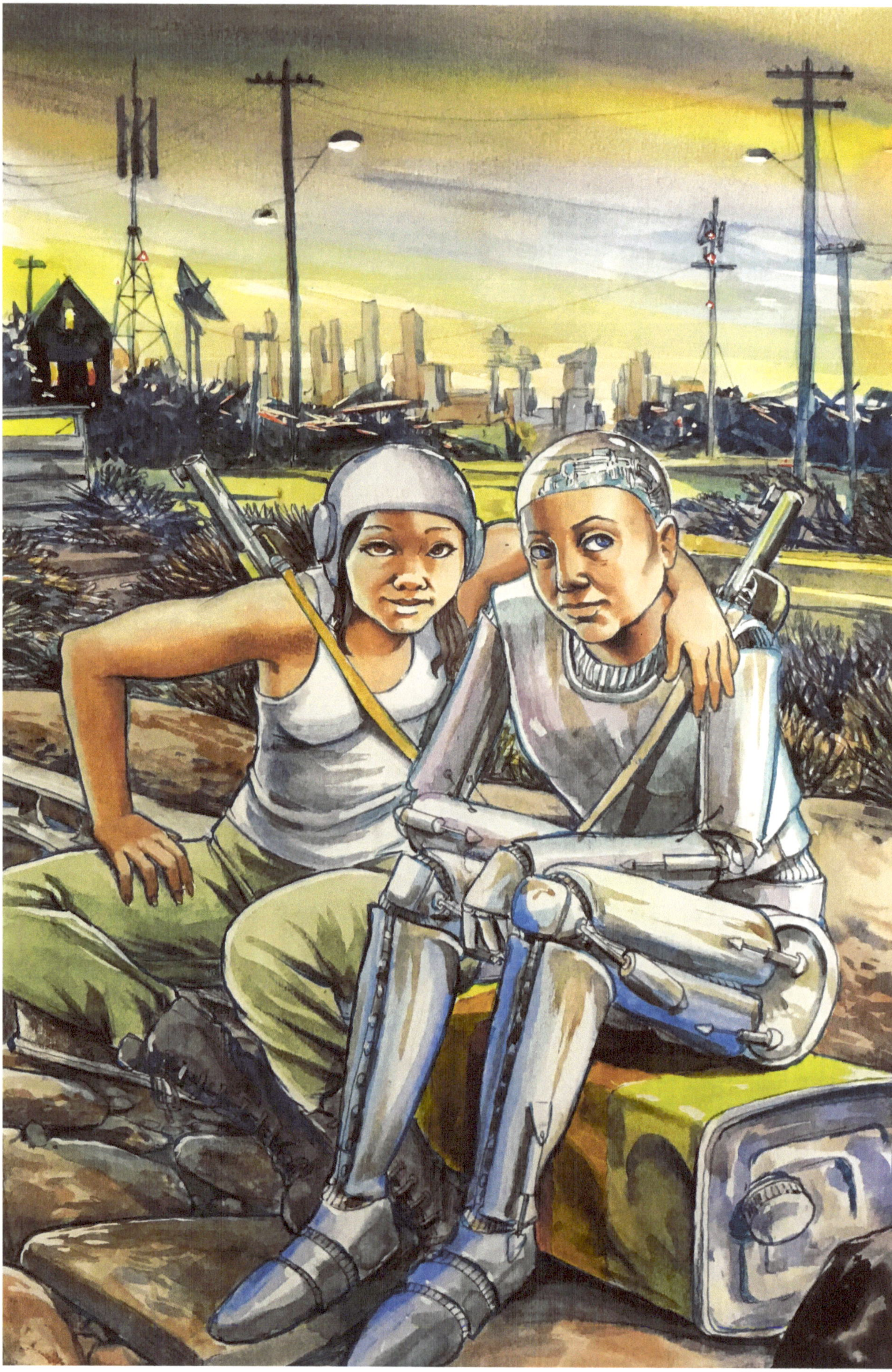

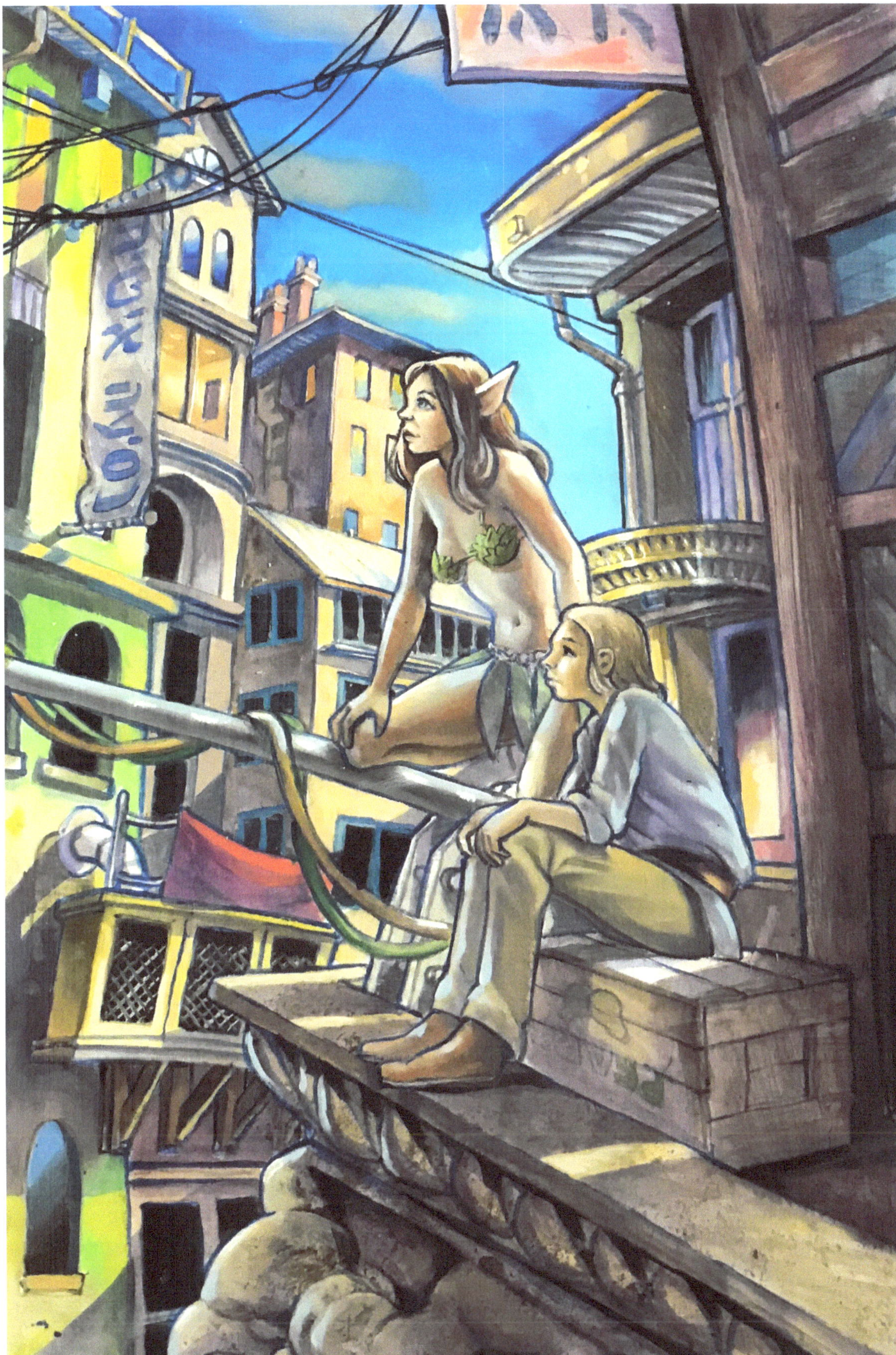

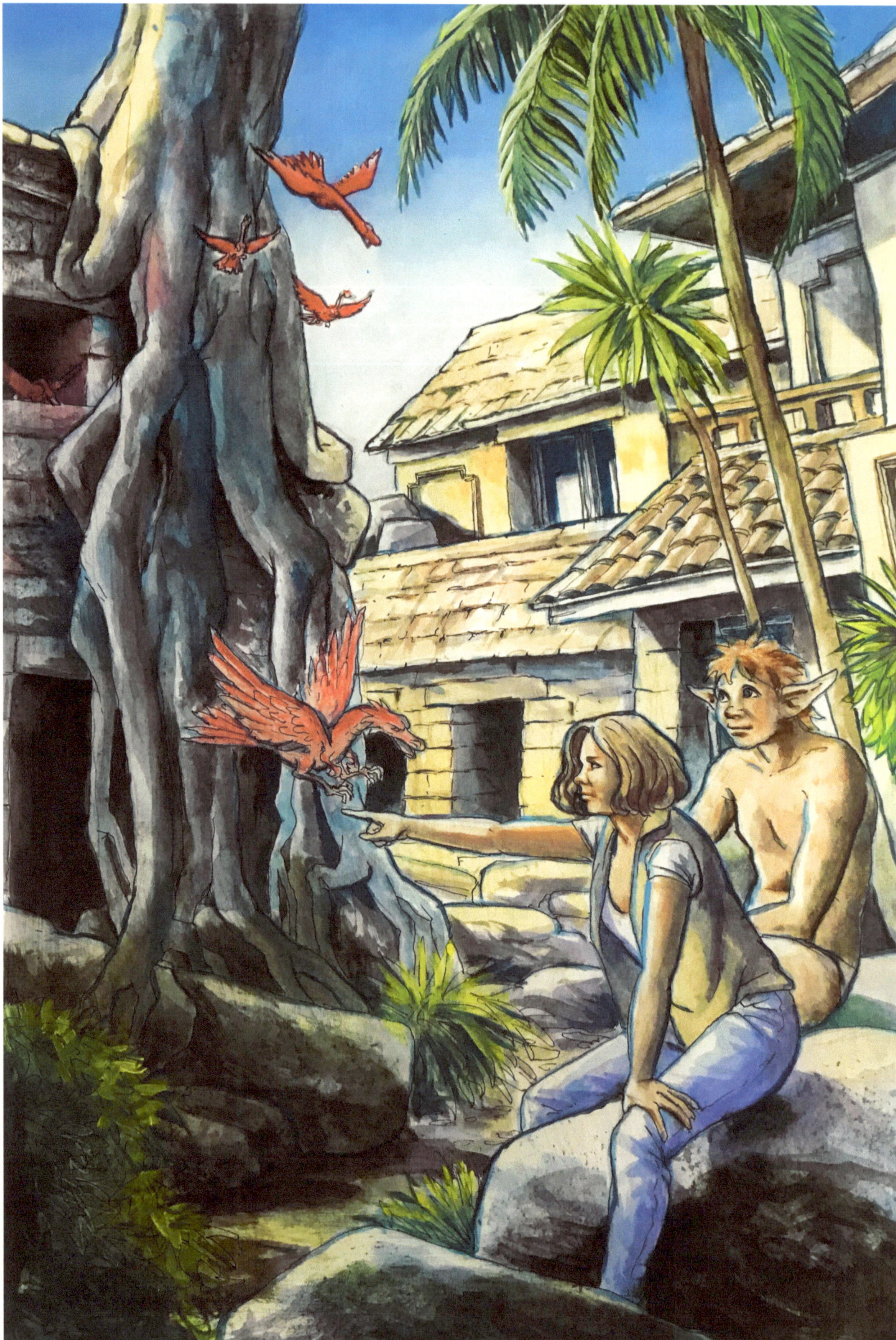

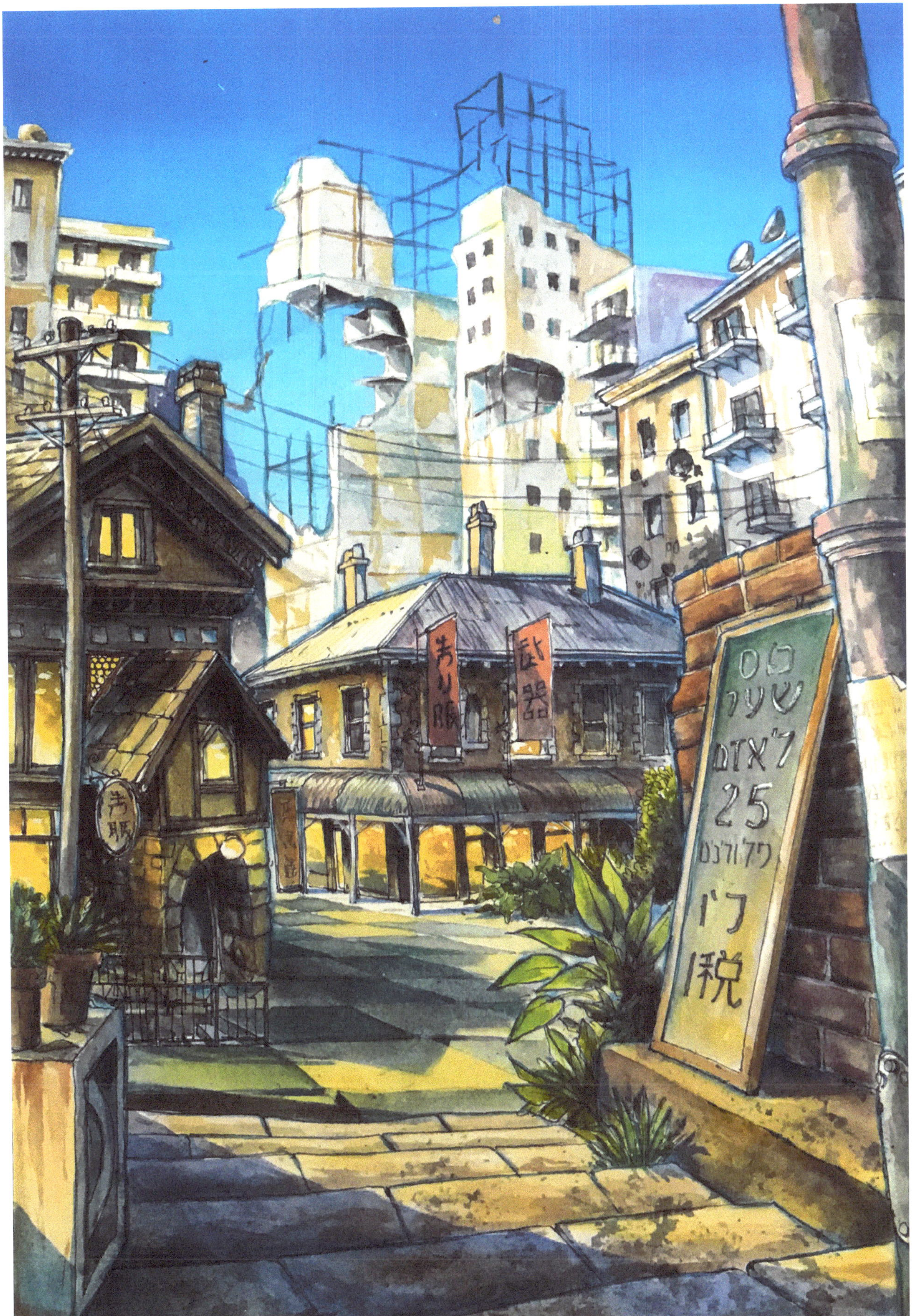
שער
25
税

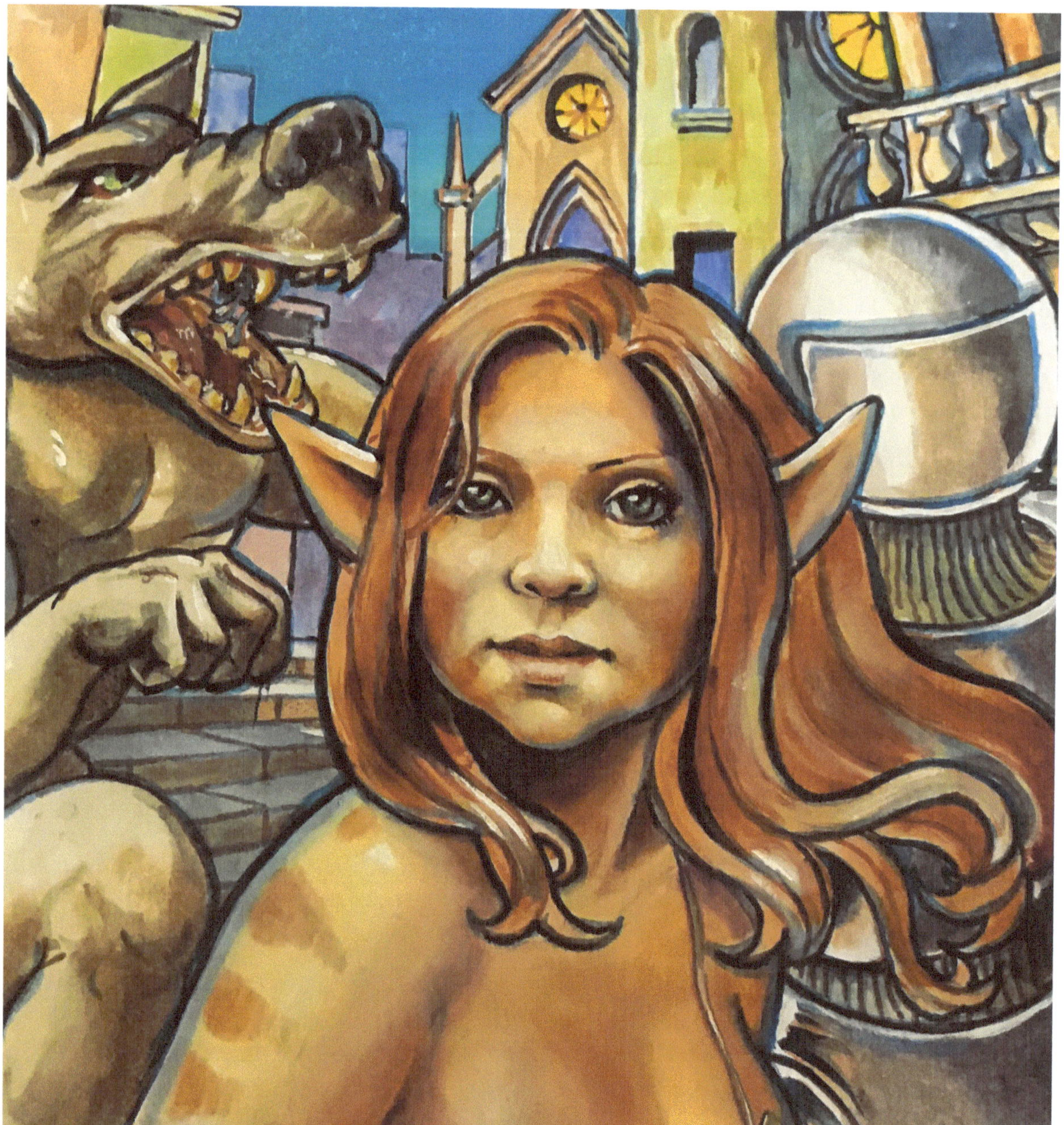

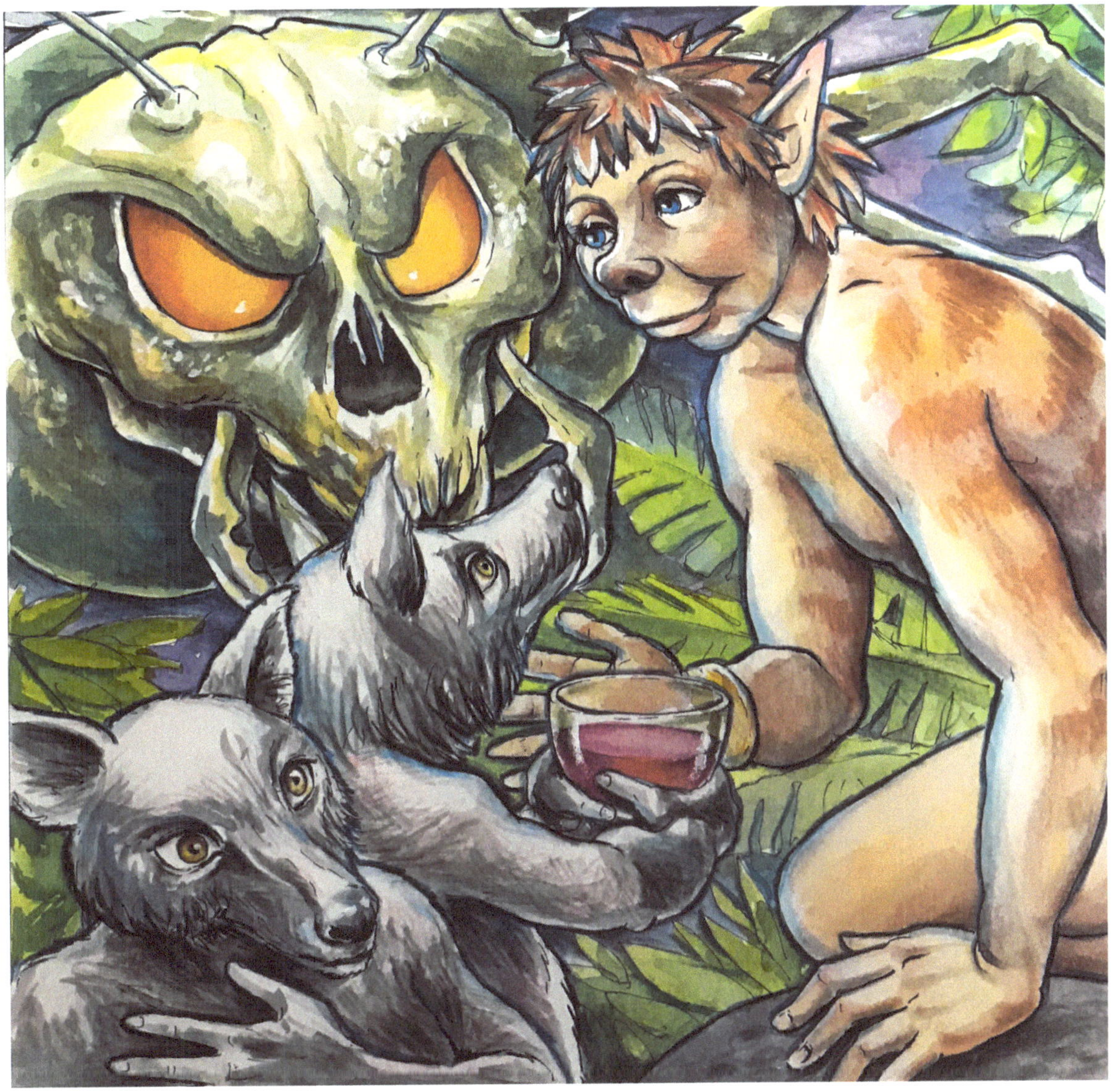

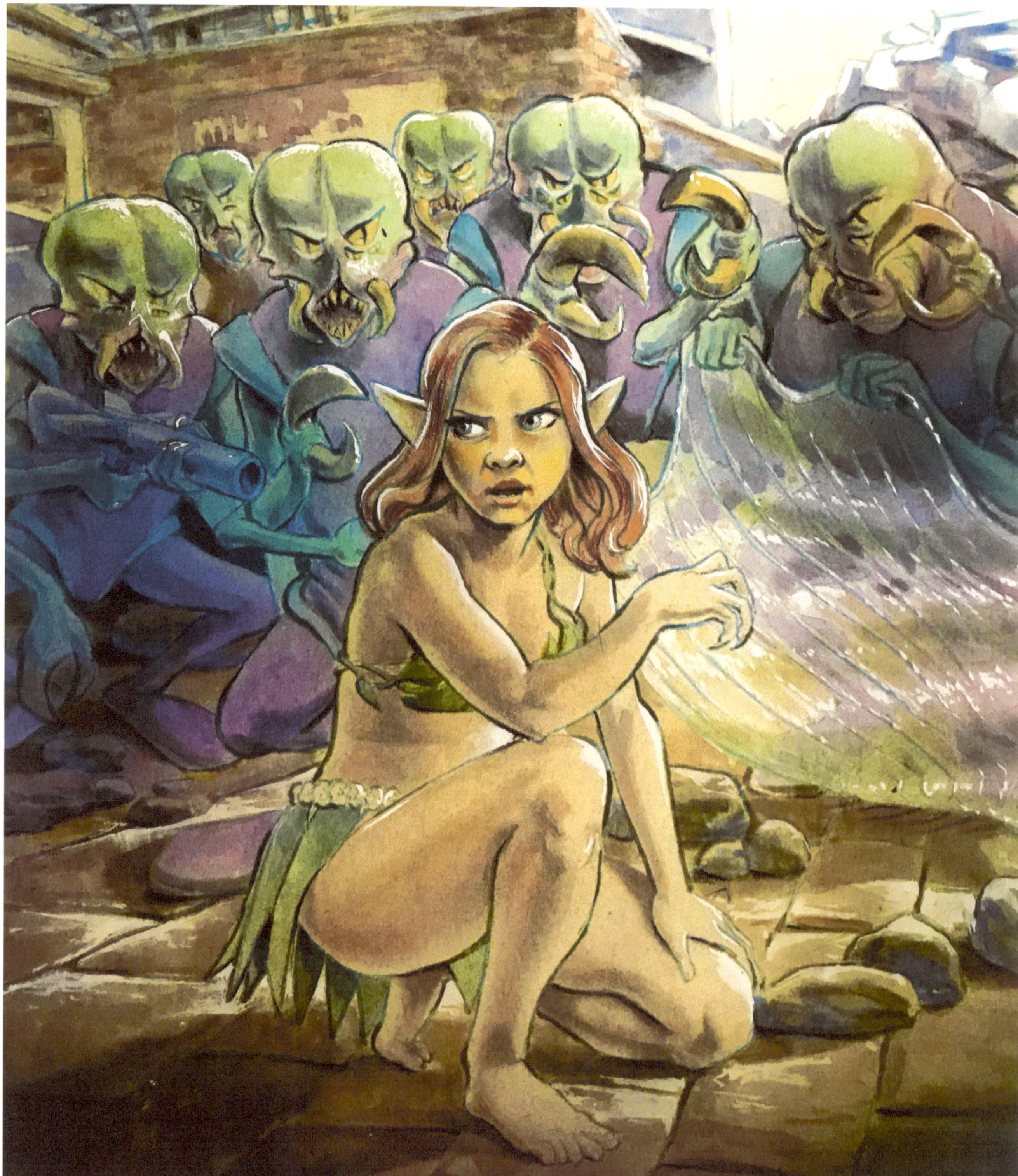

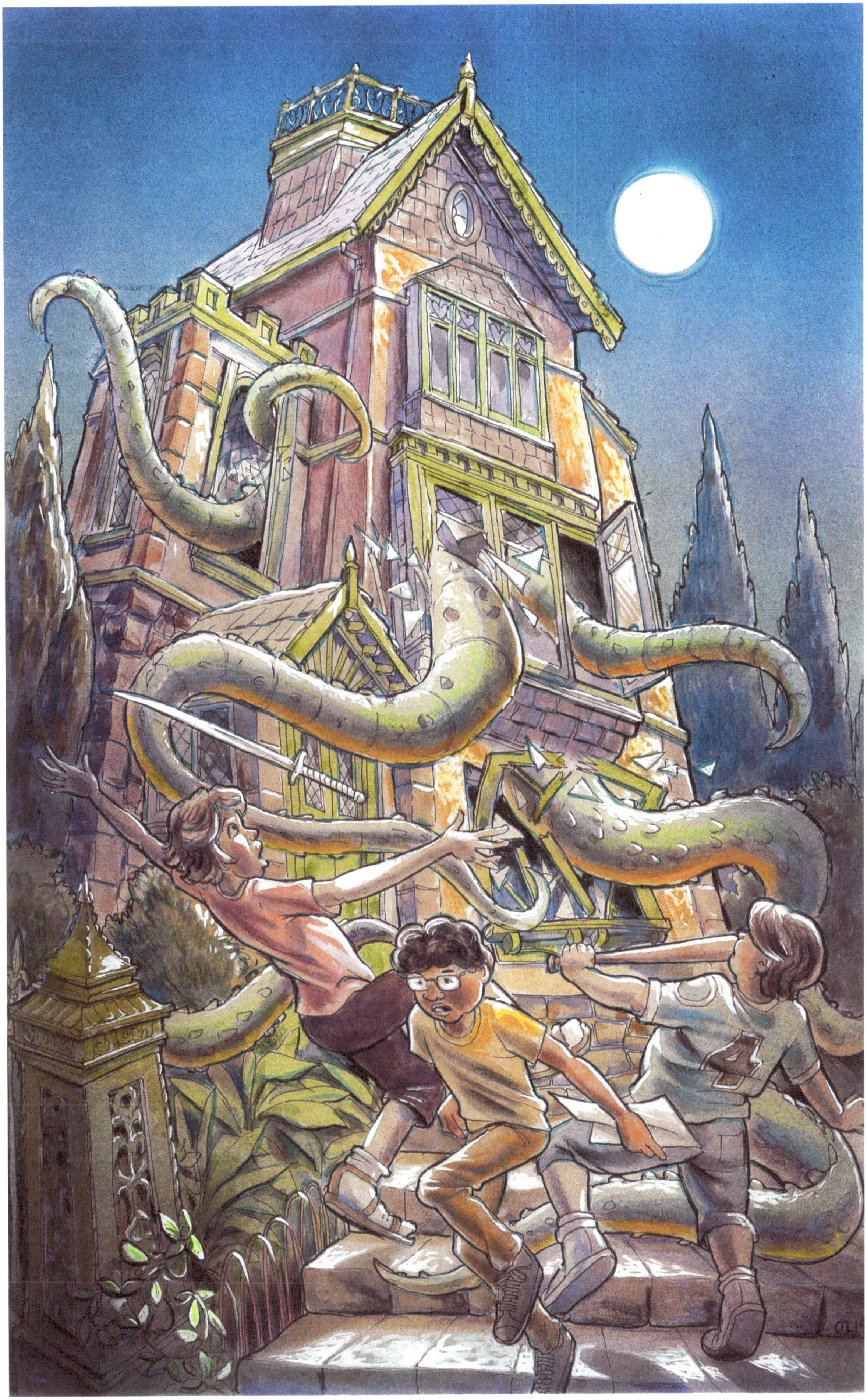

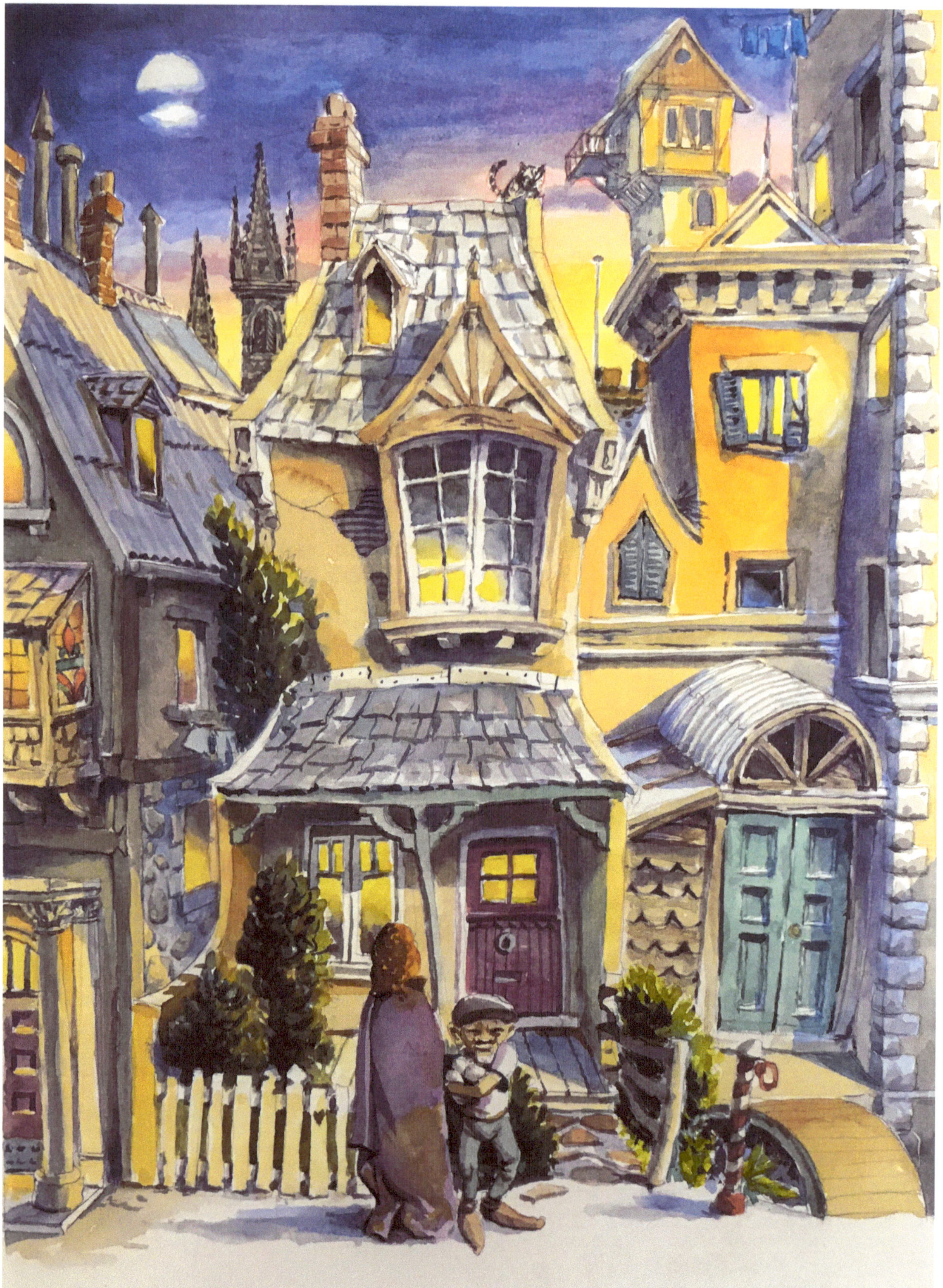

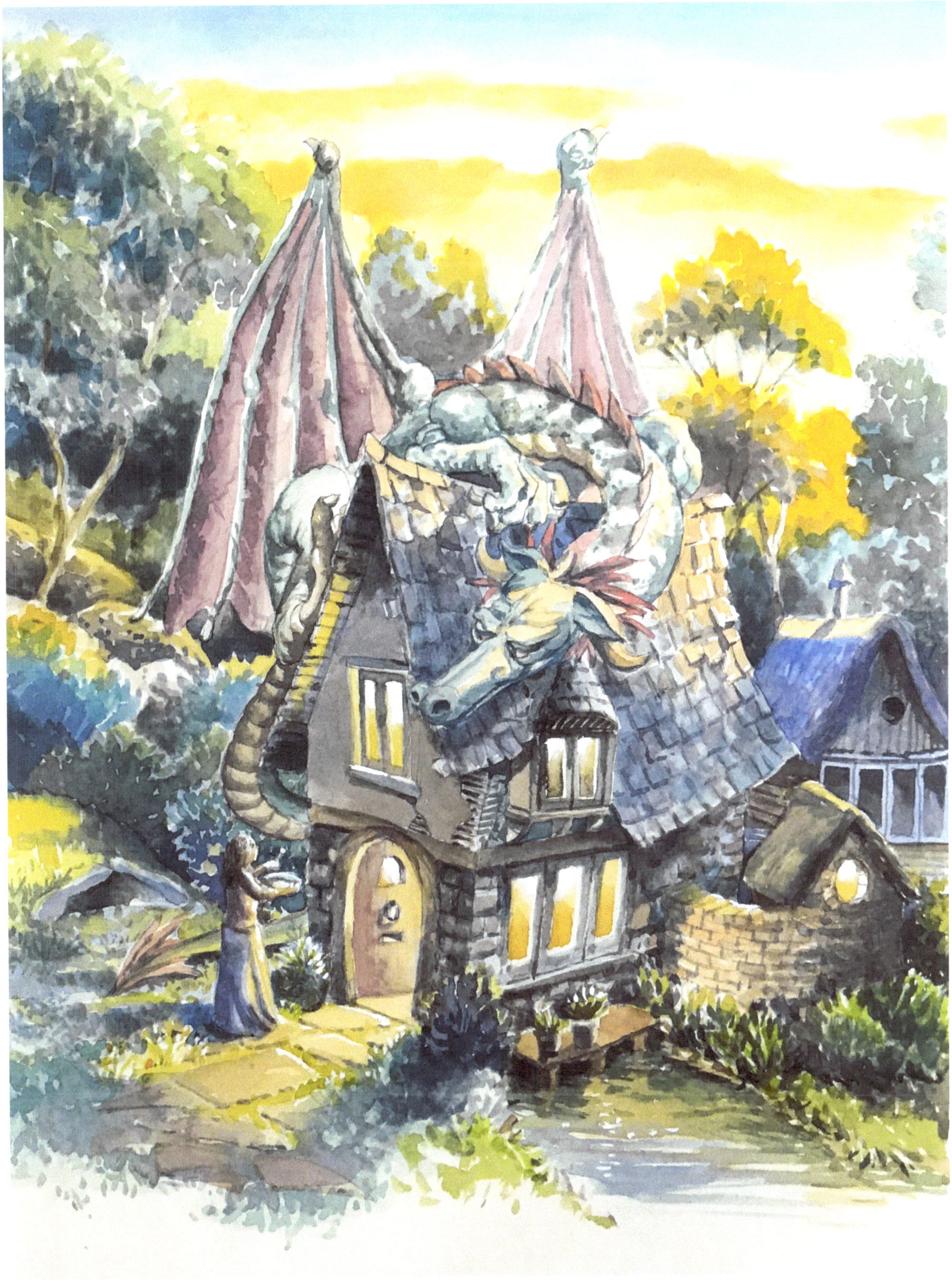

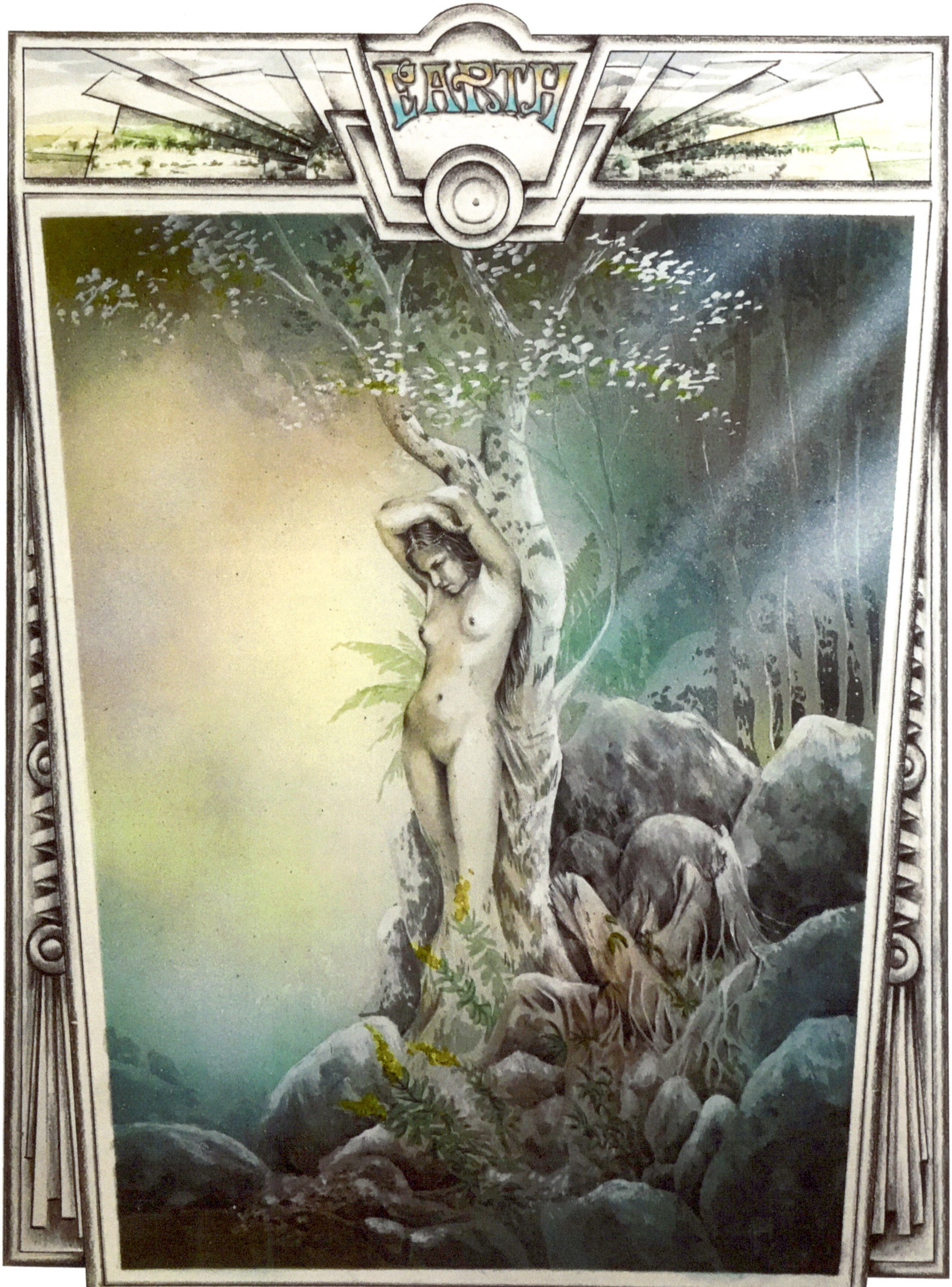
EARTH

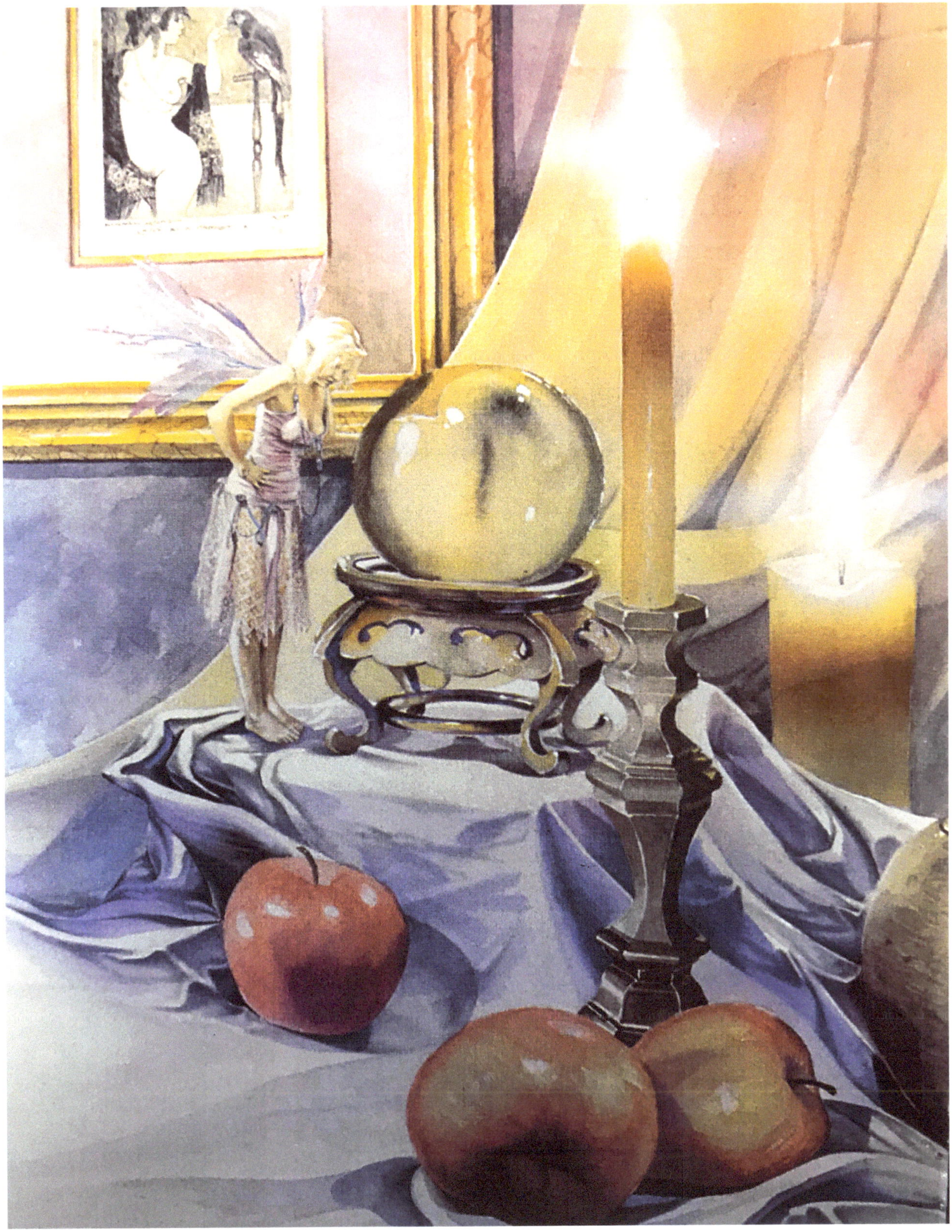

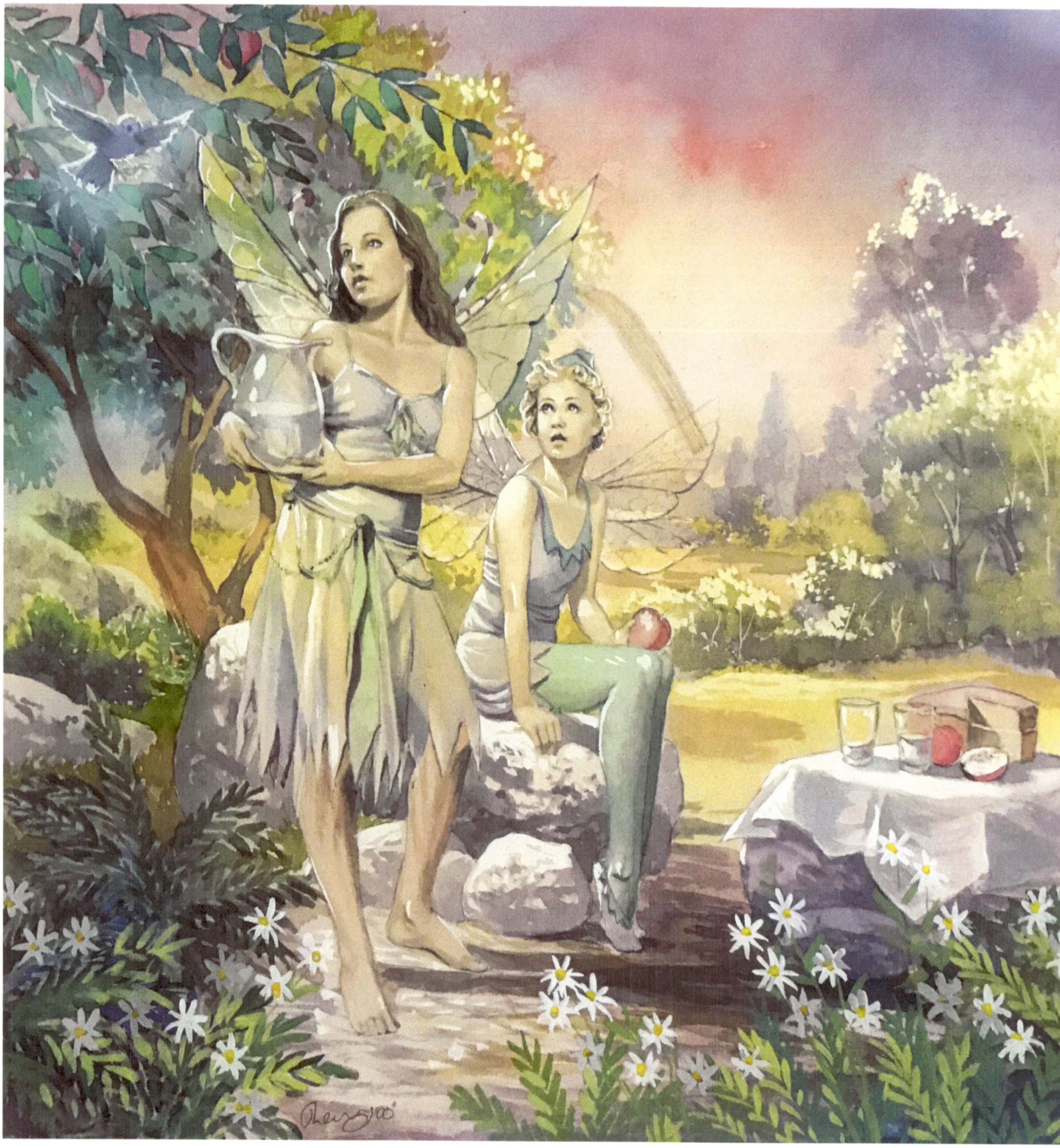

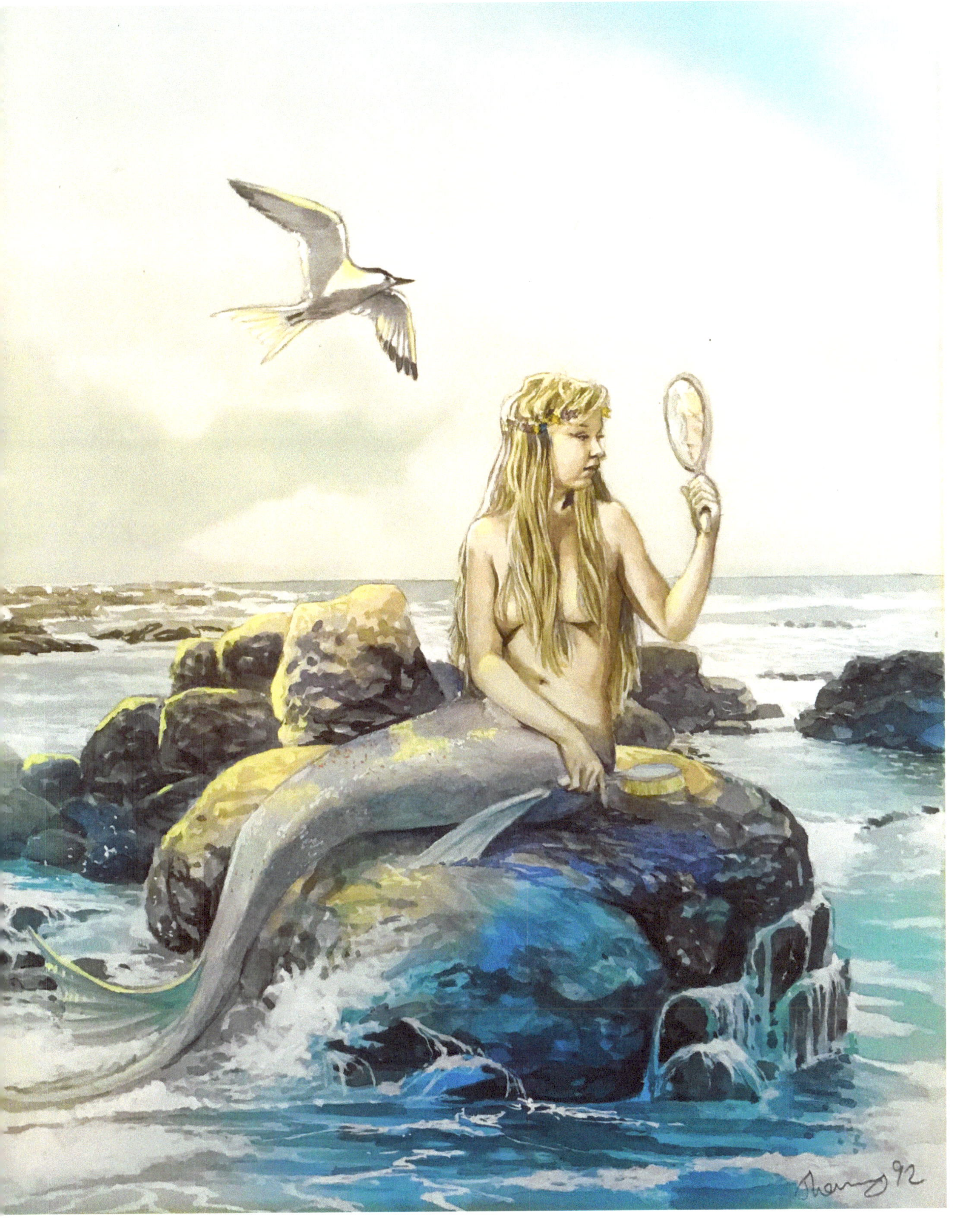

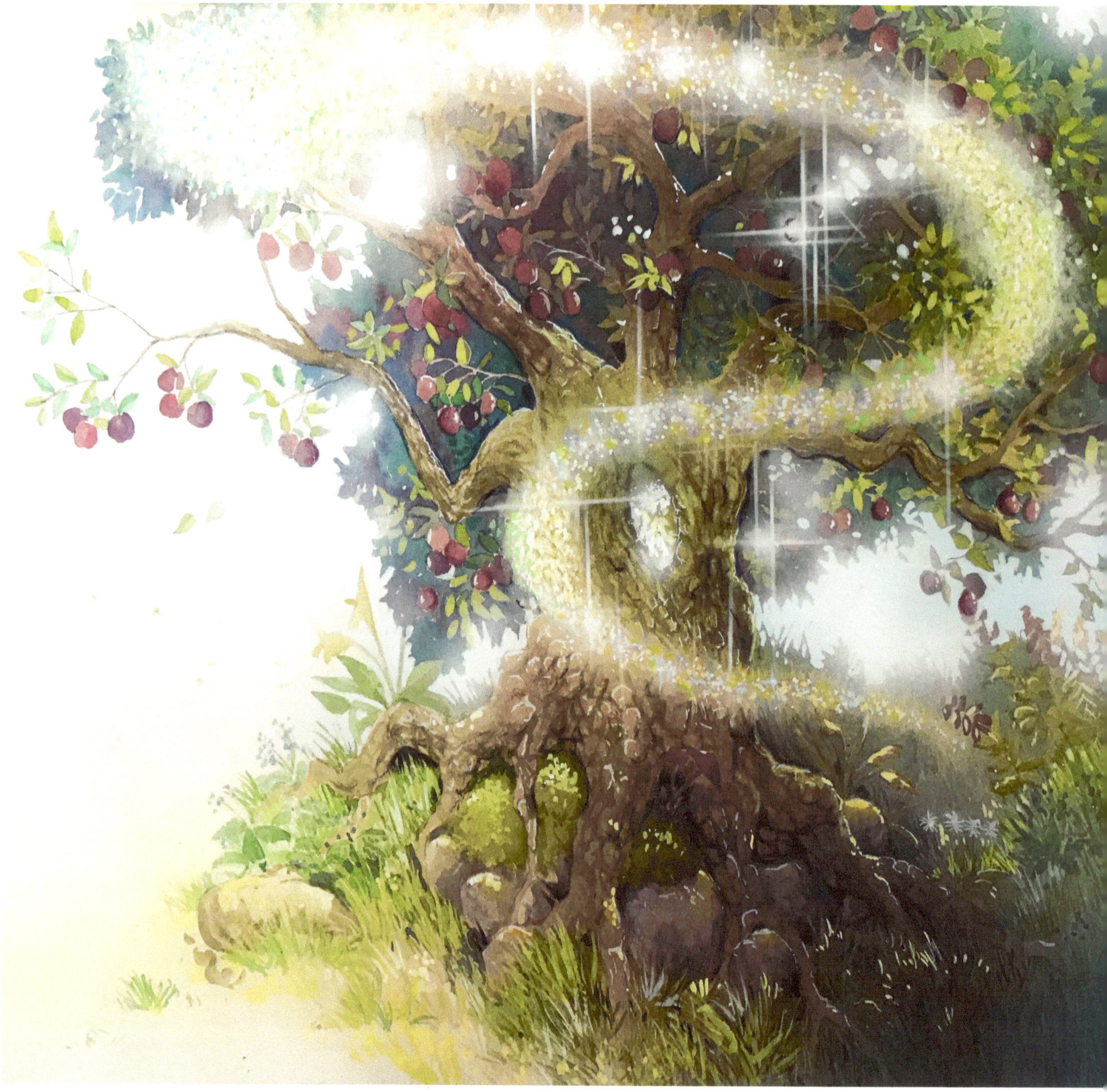

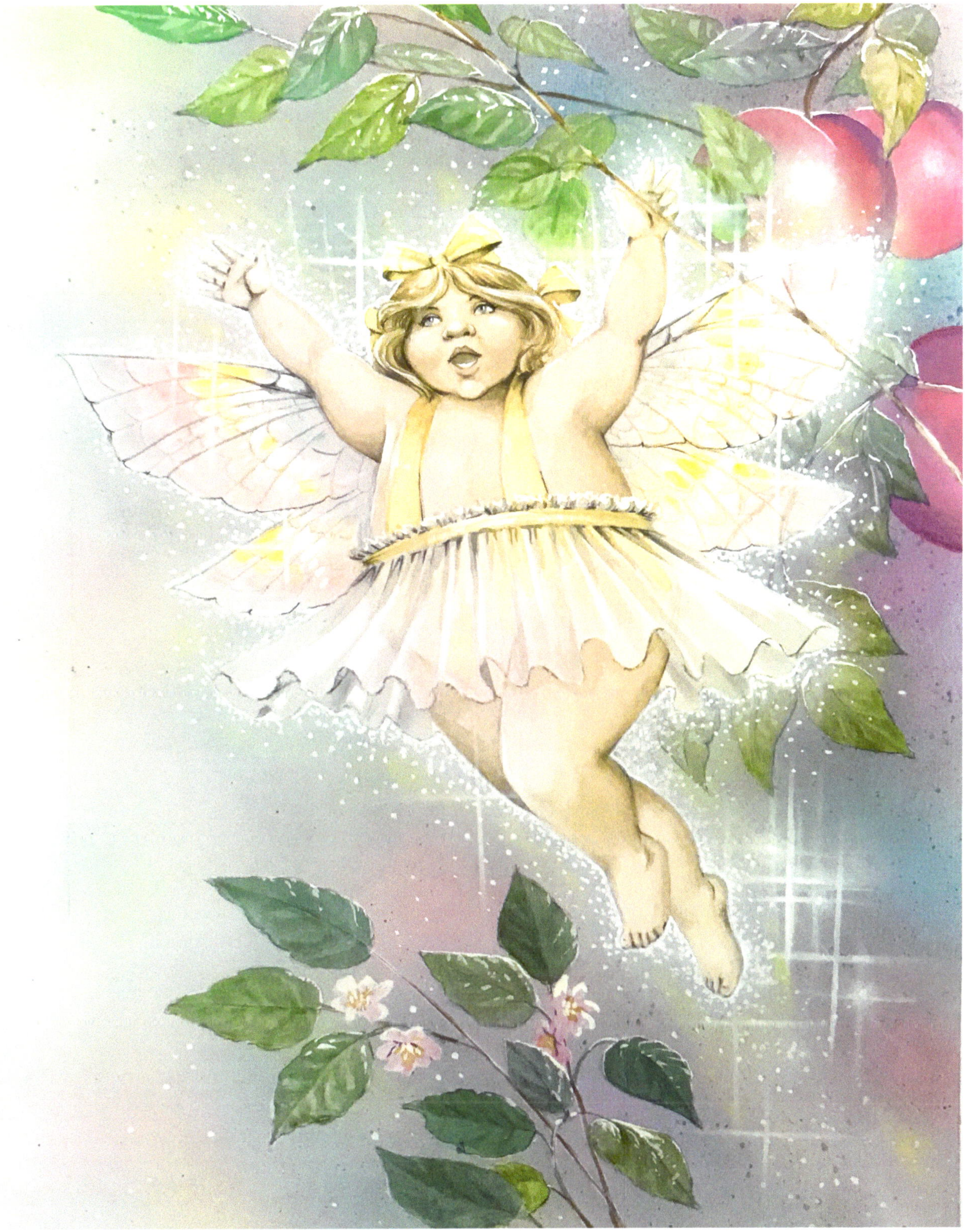

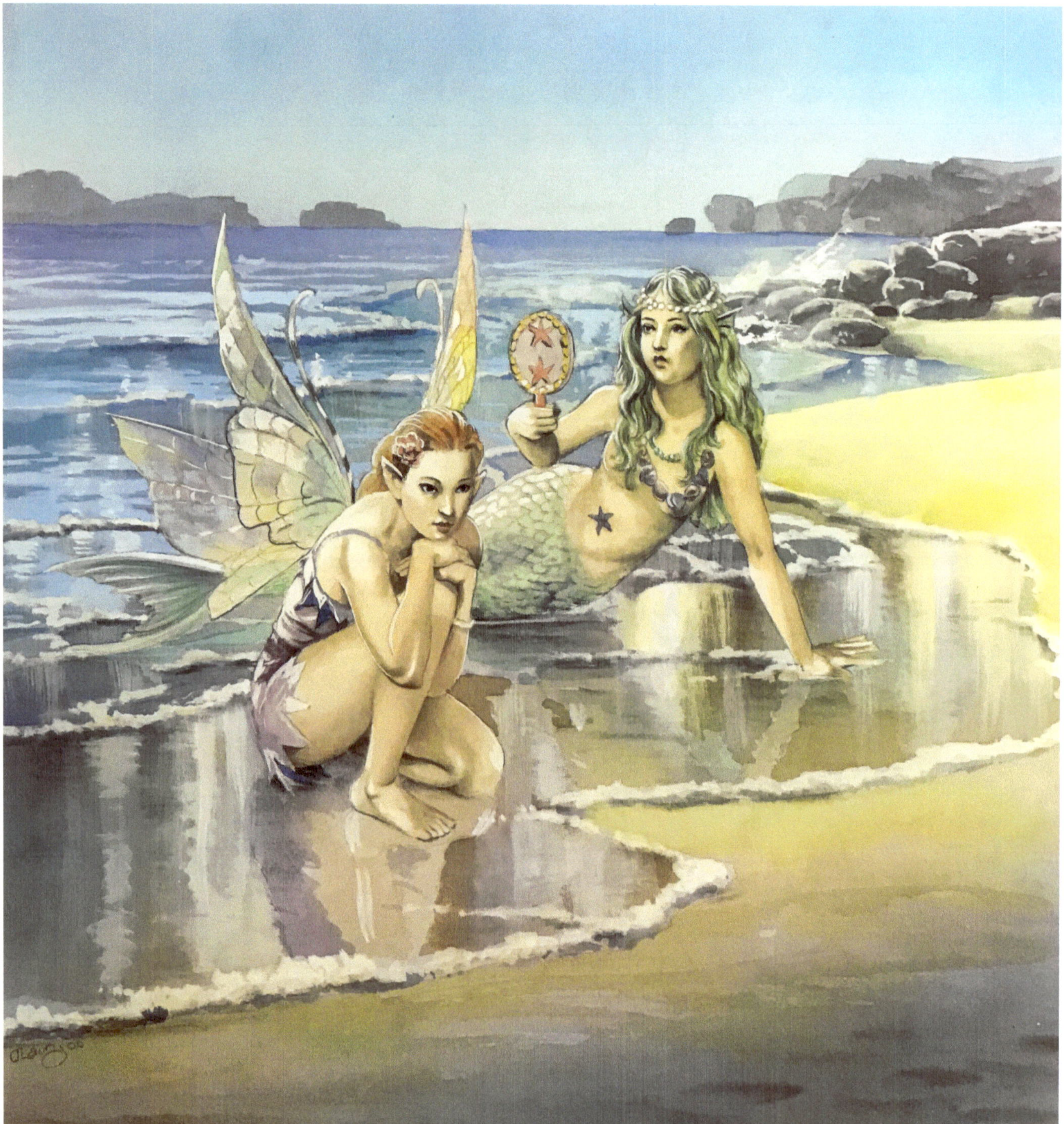

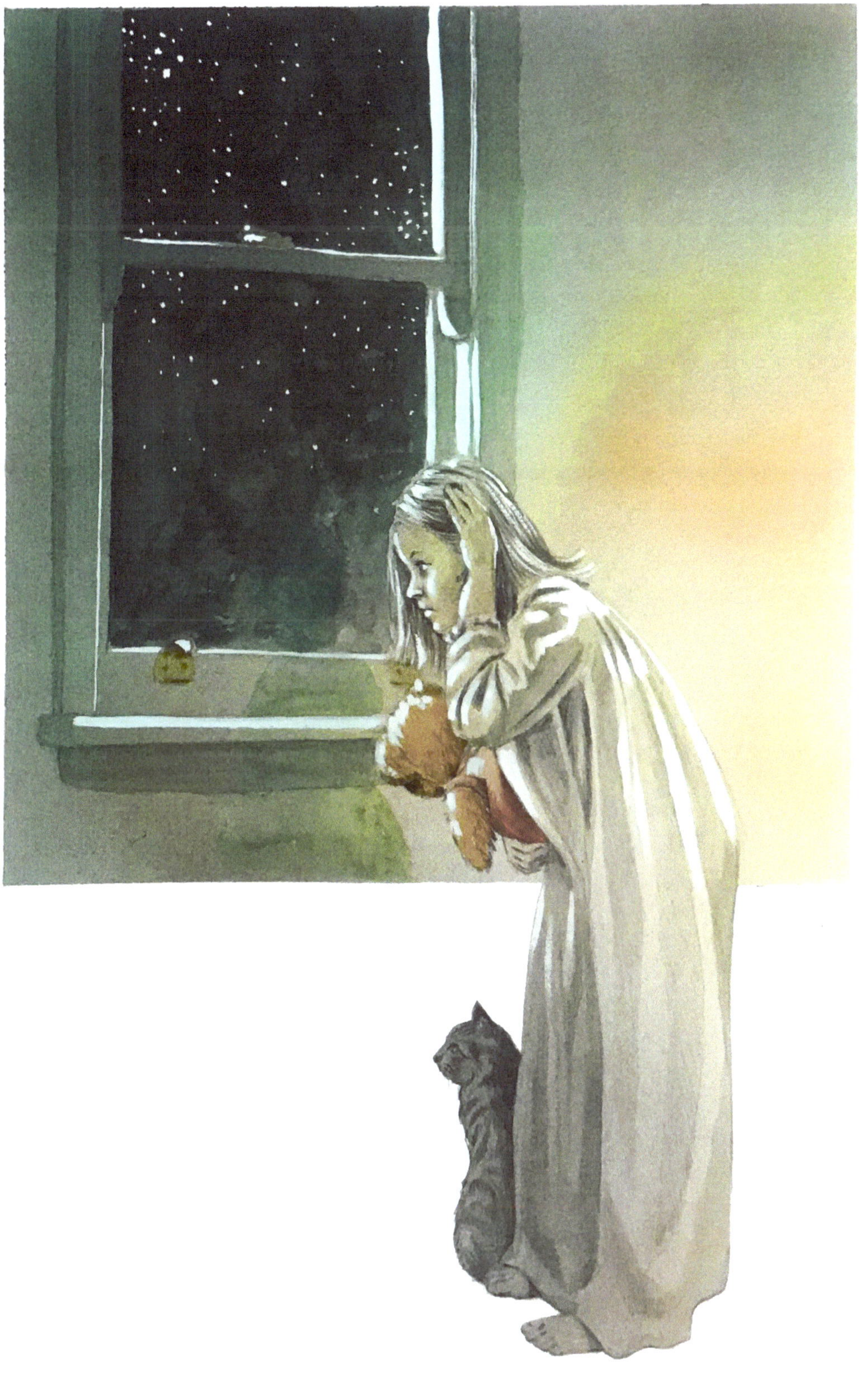

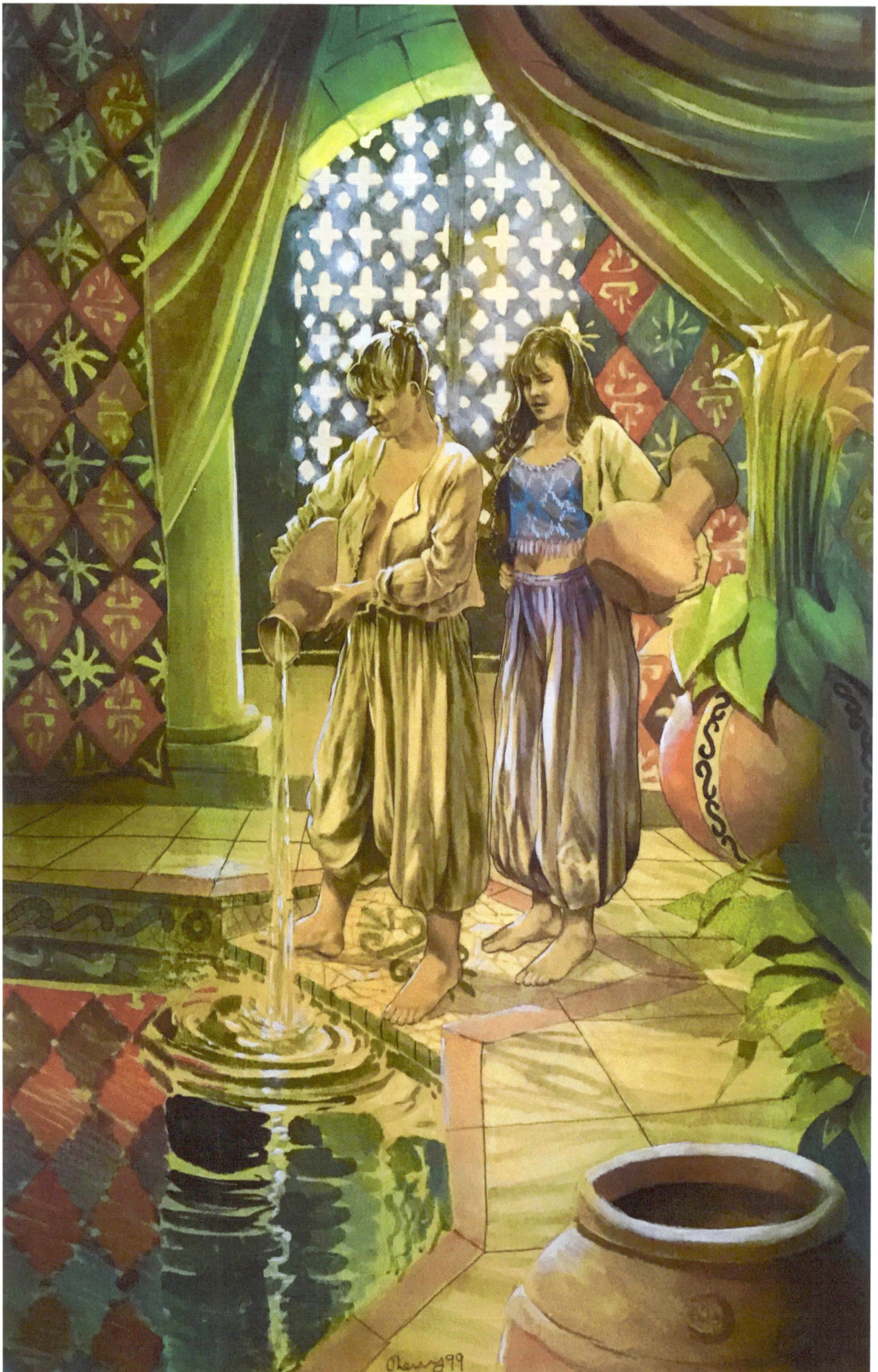

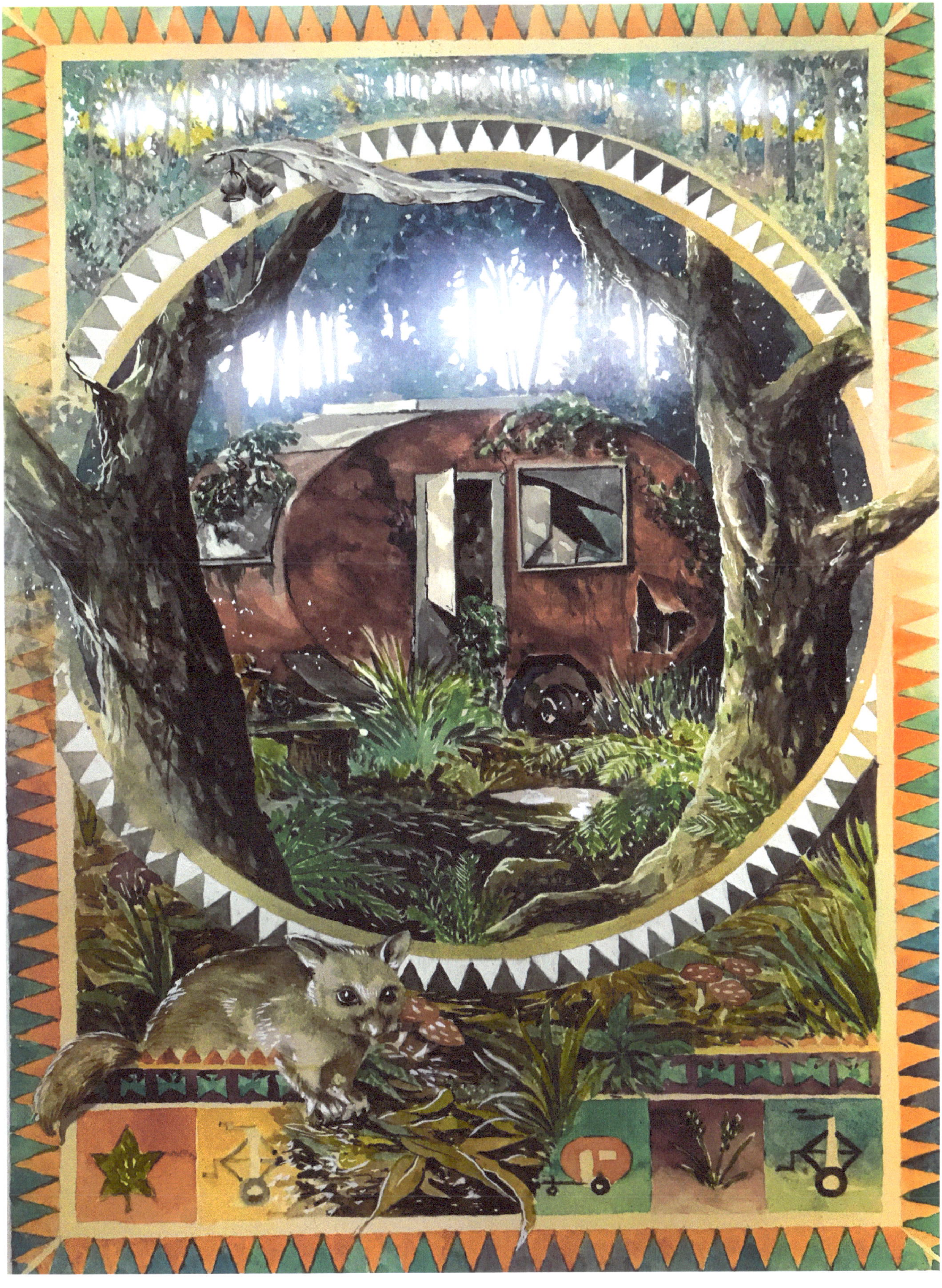

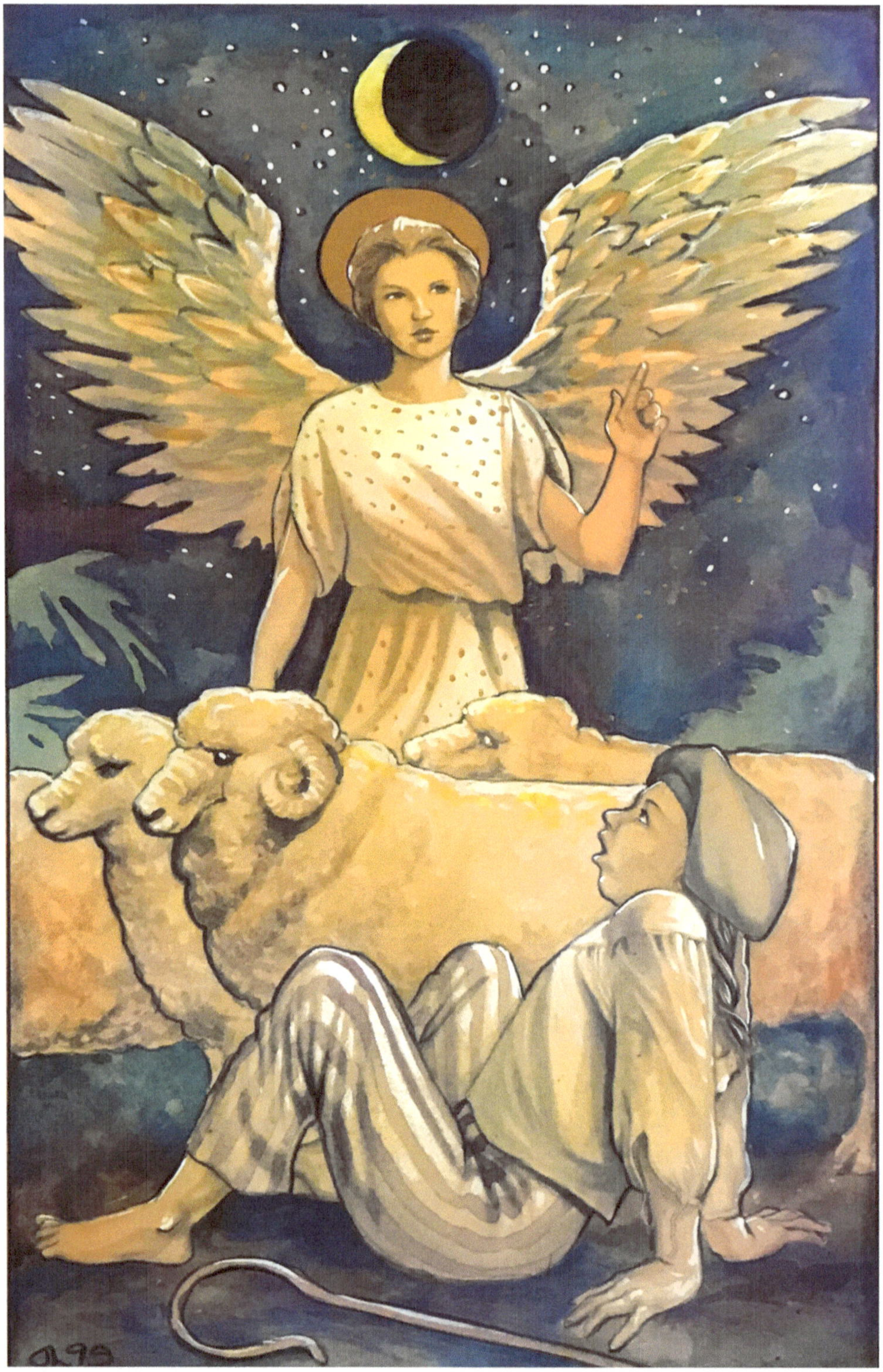

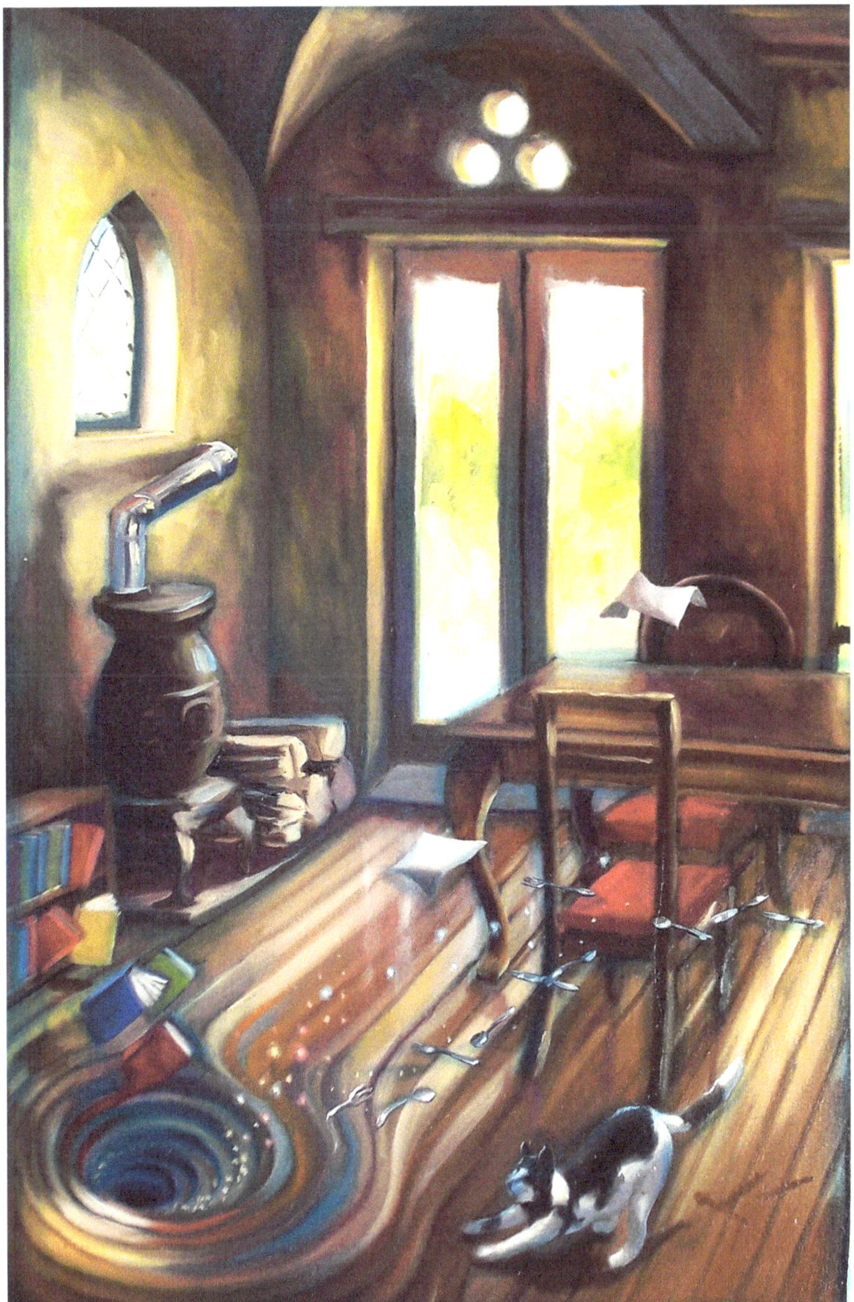

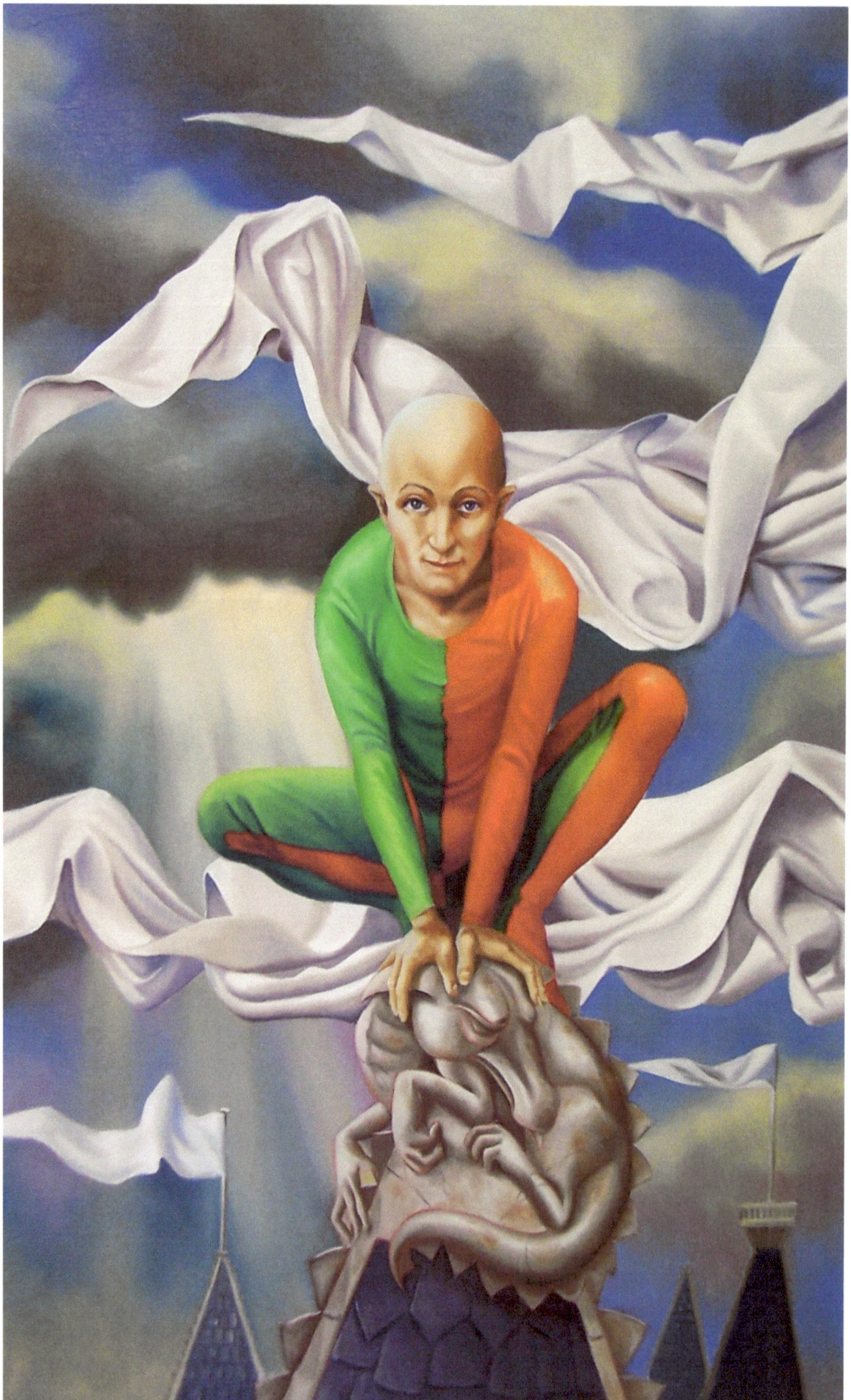

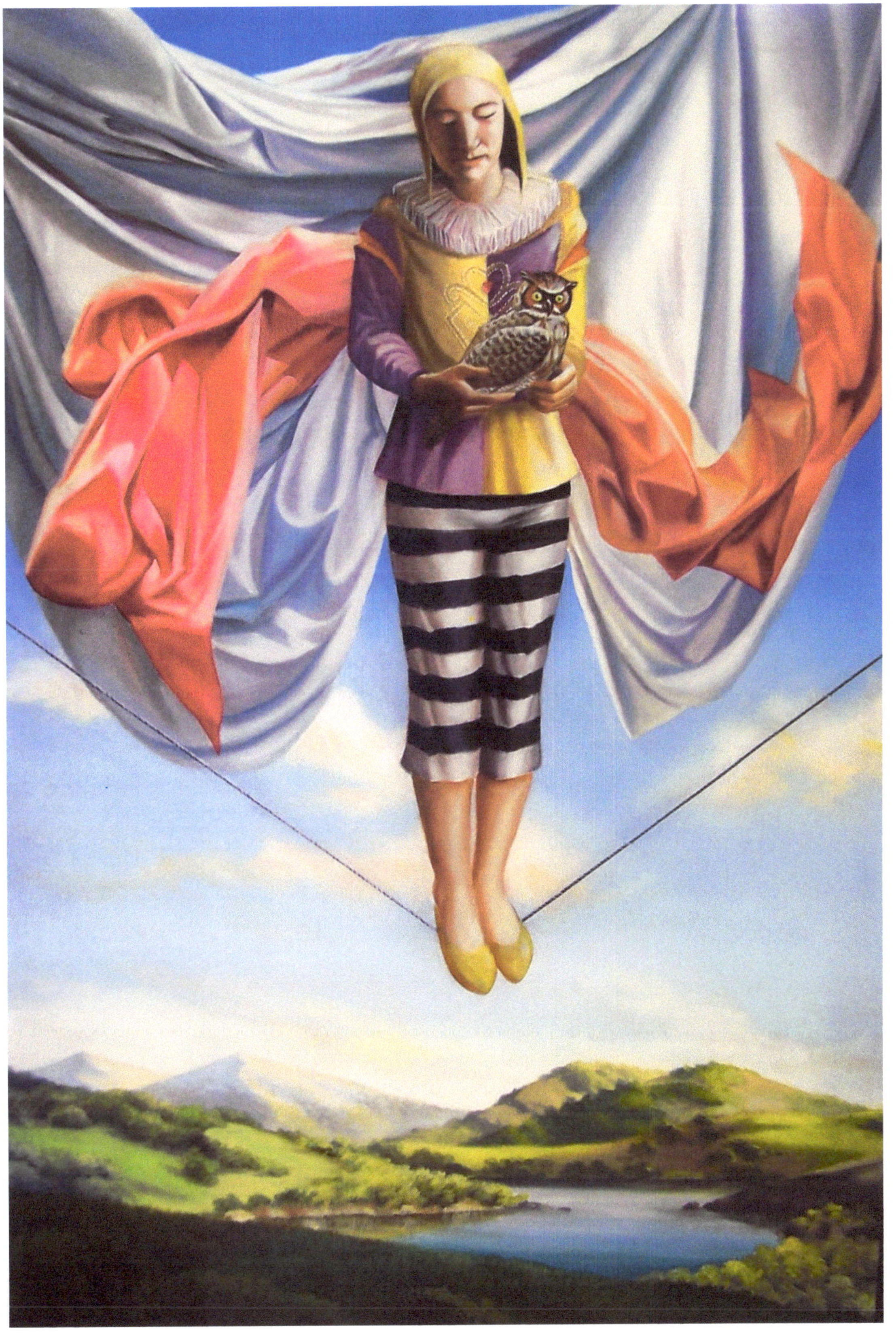

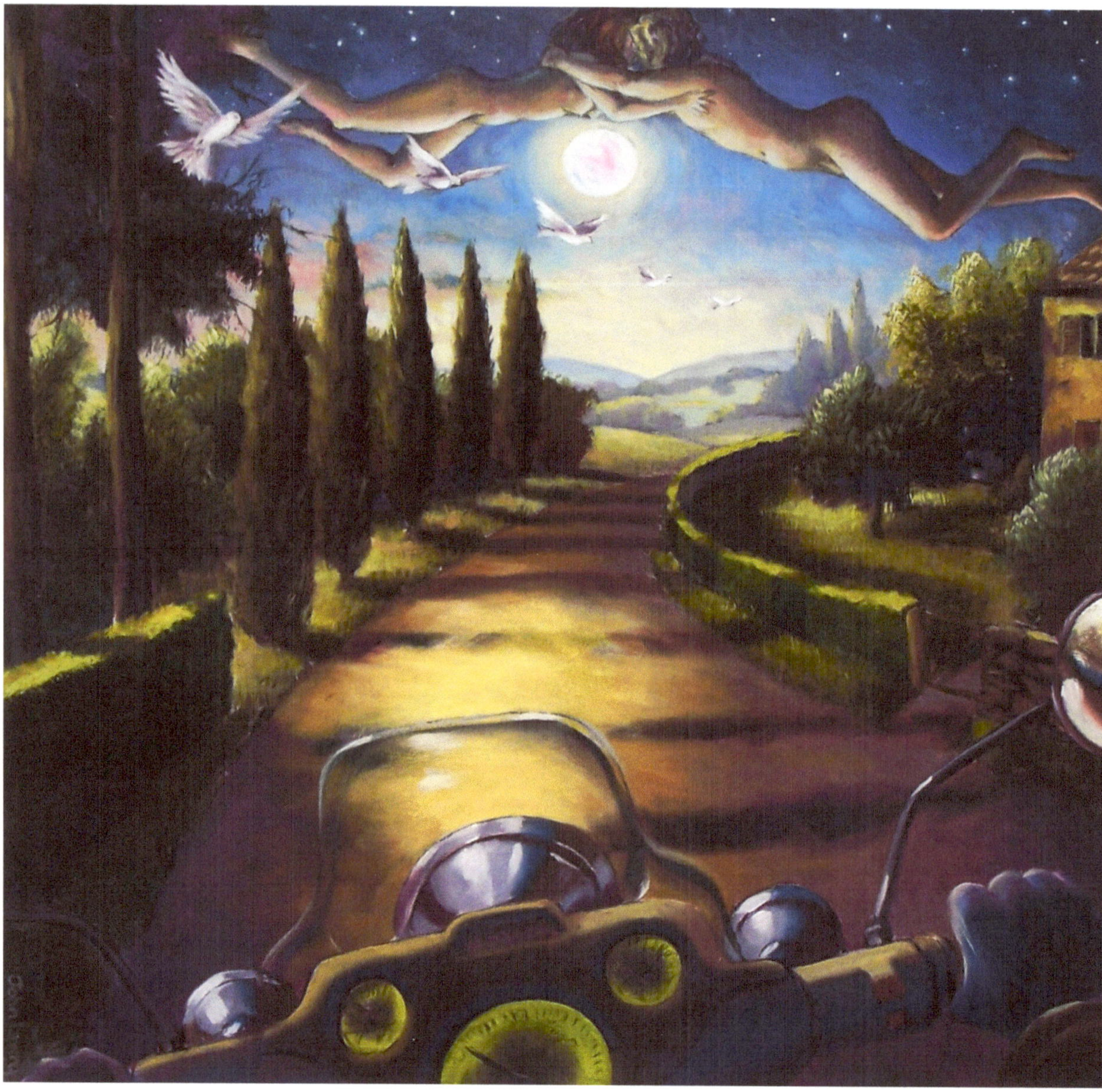

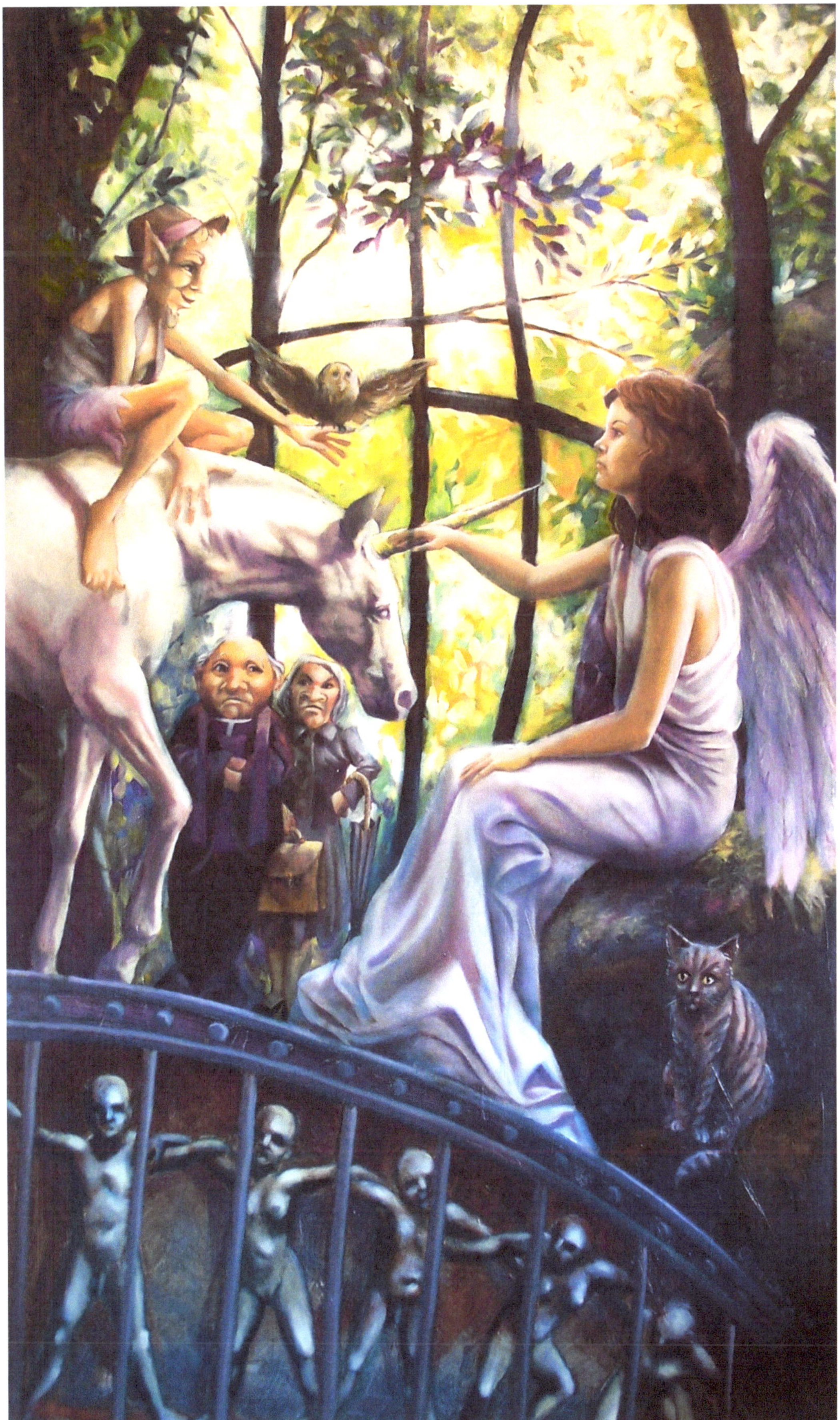

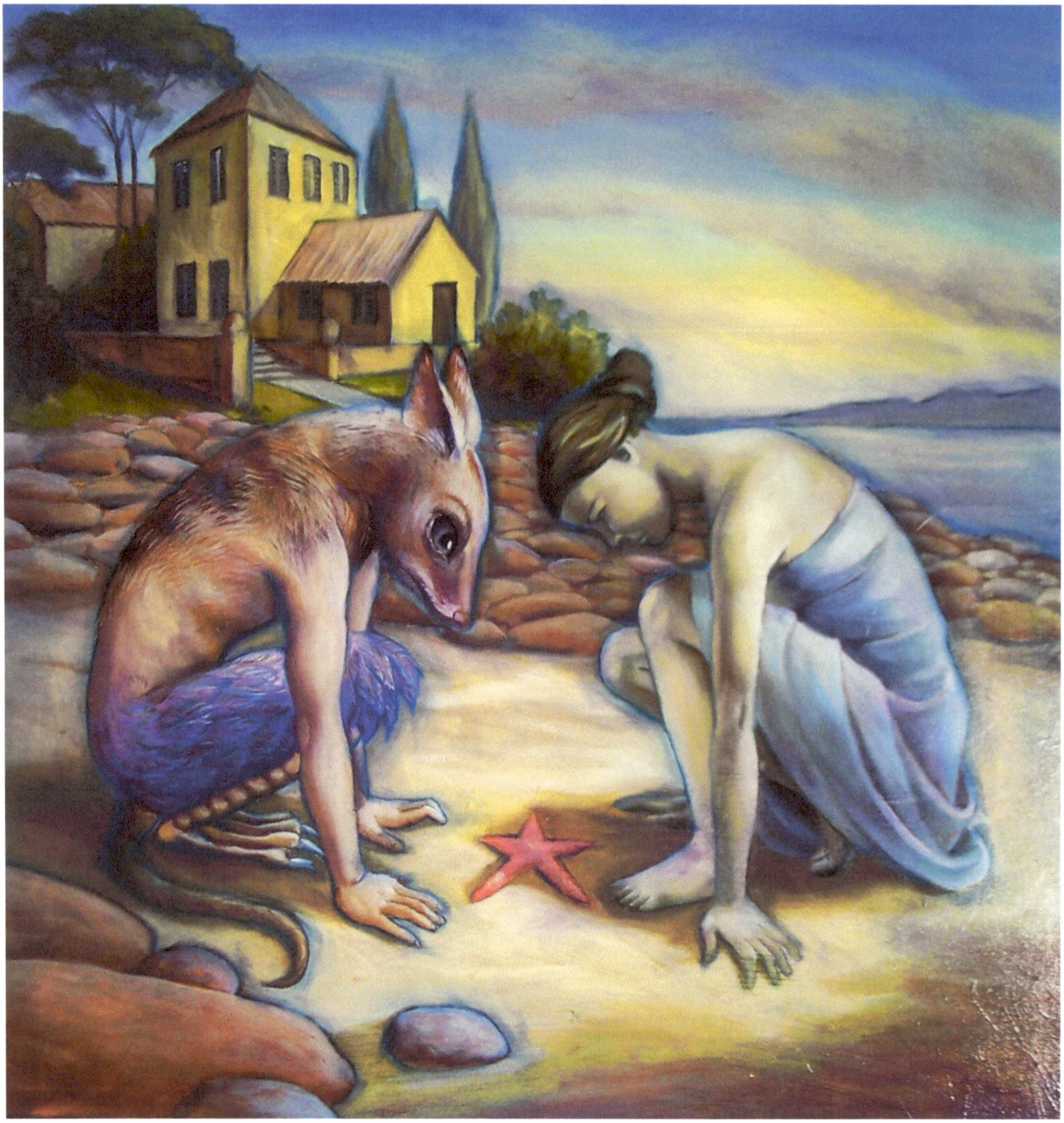

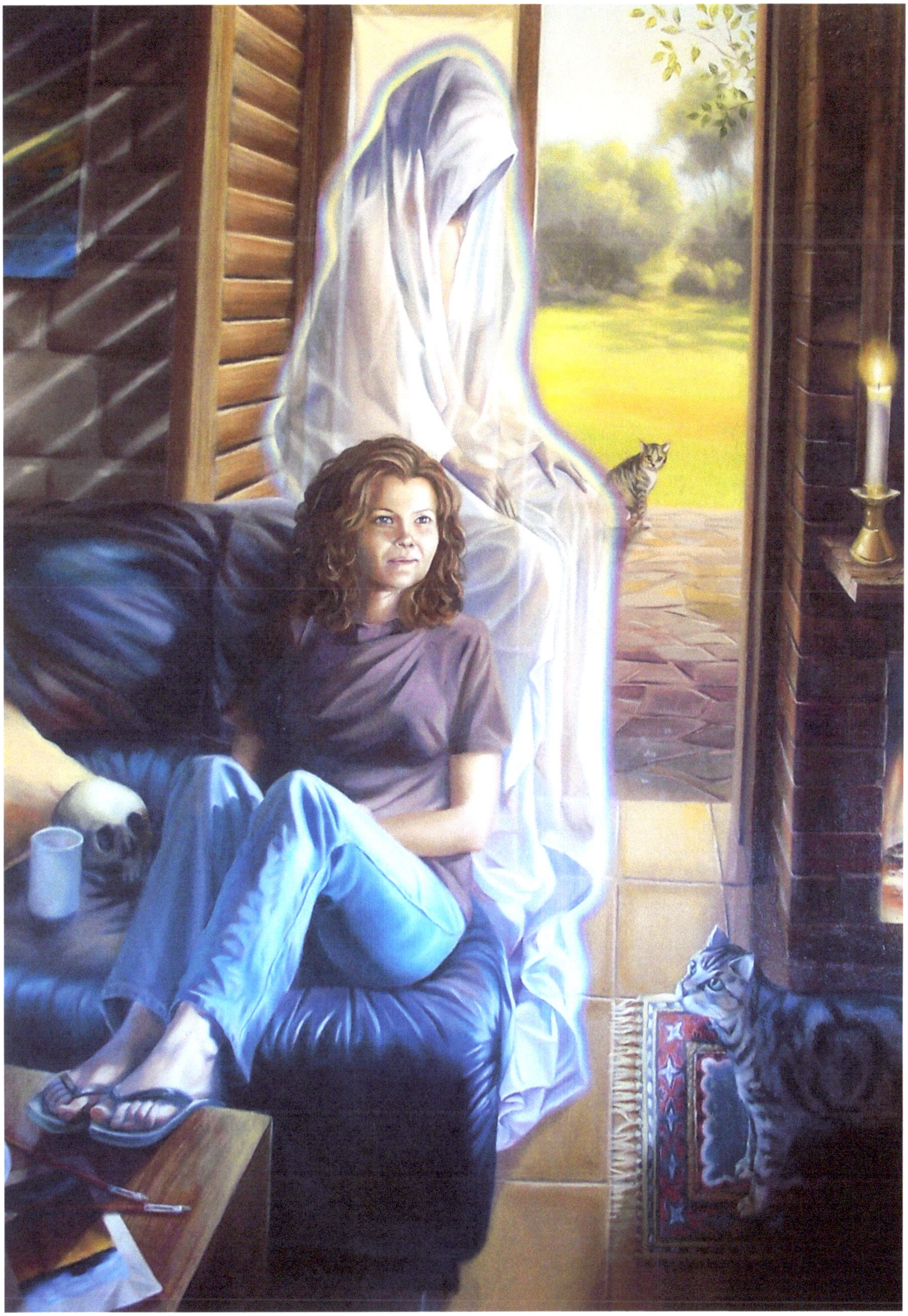

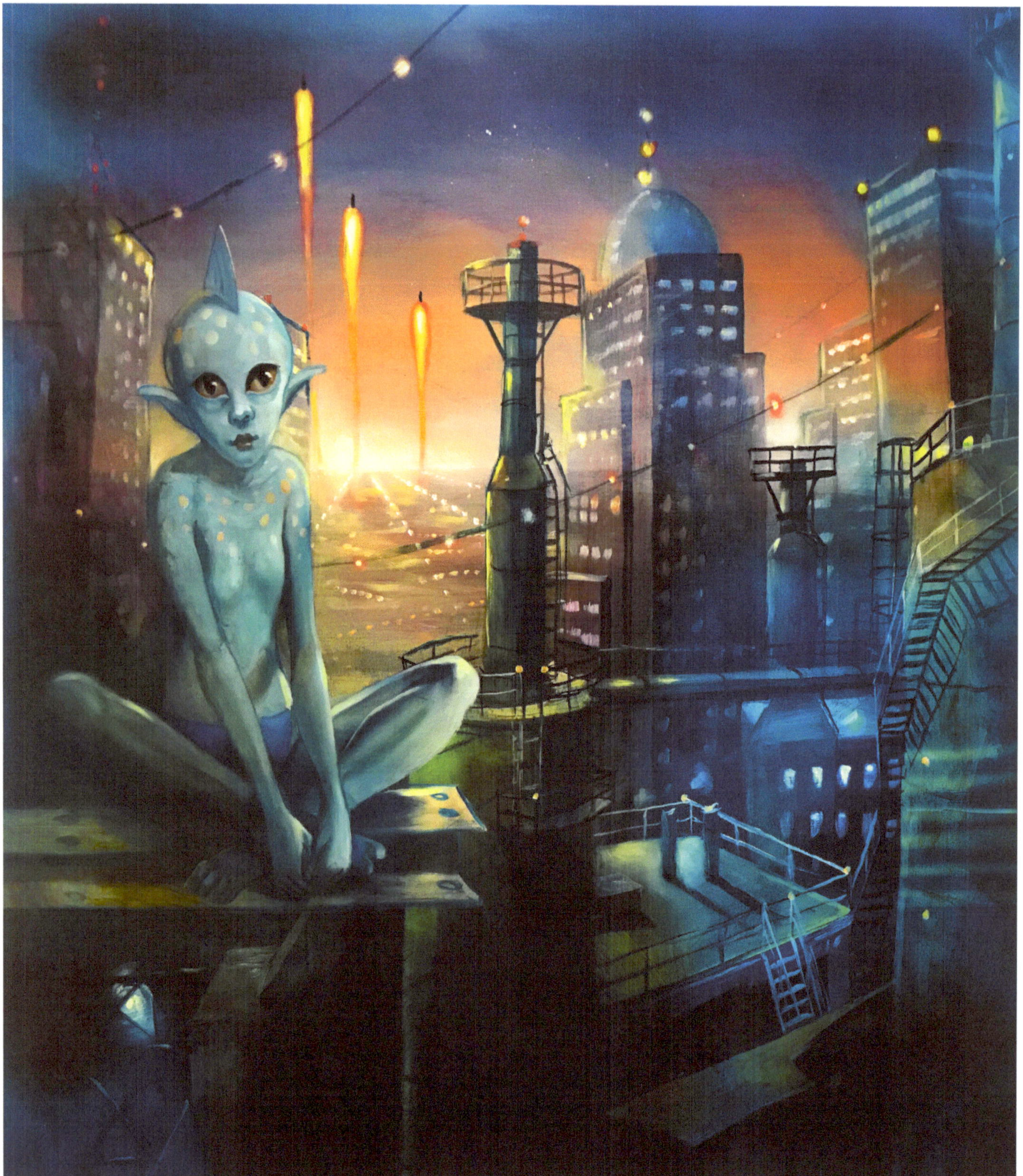

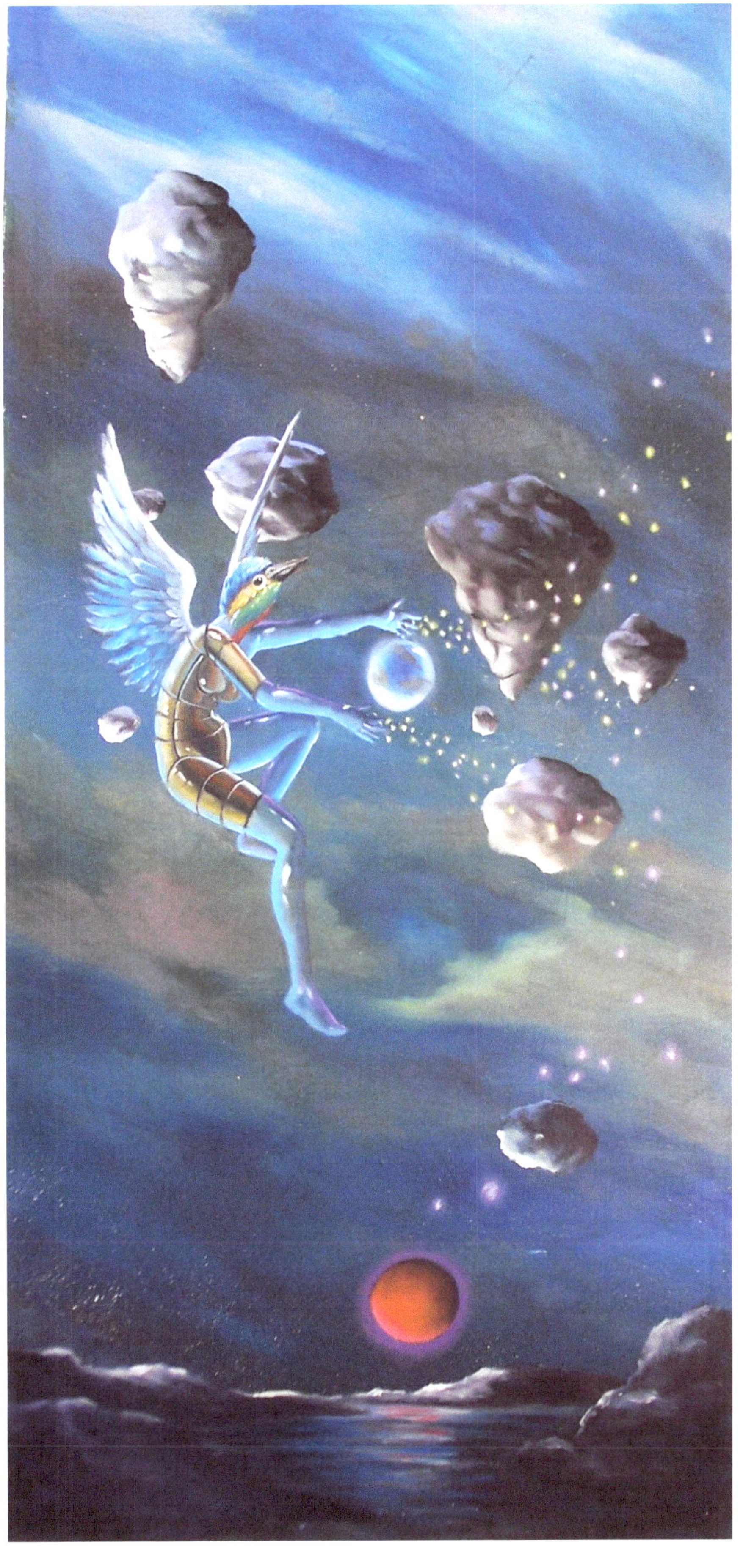

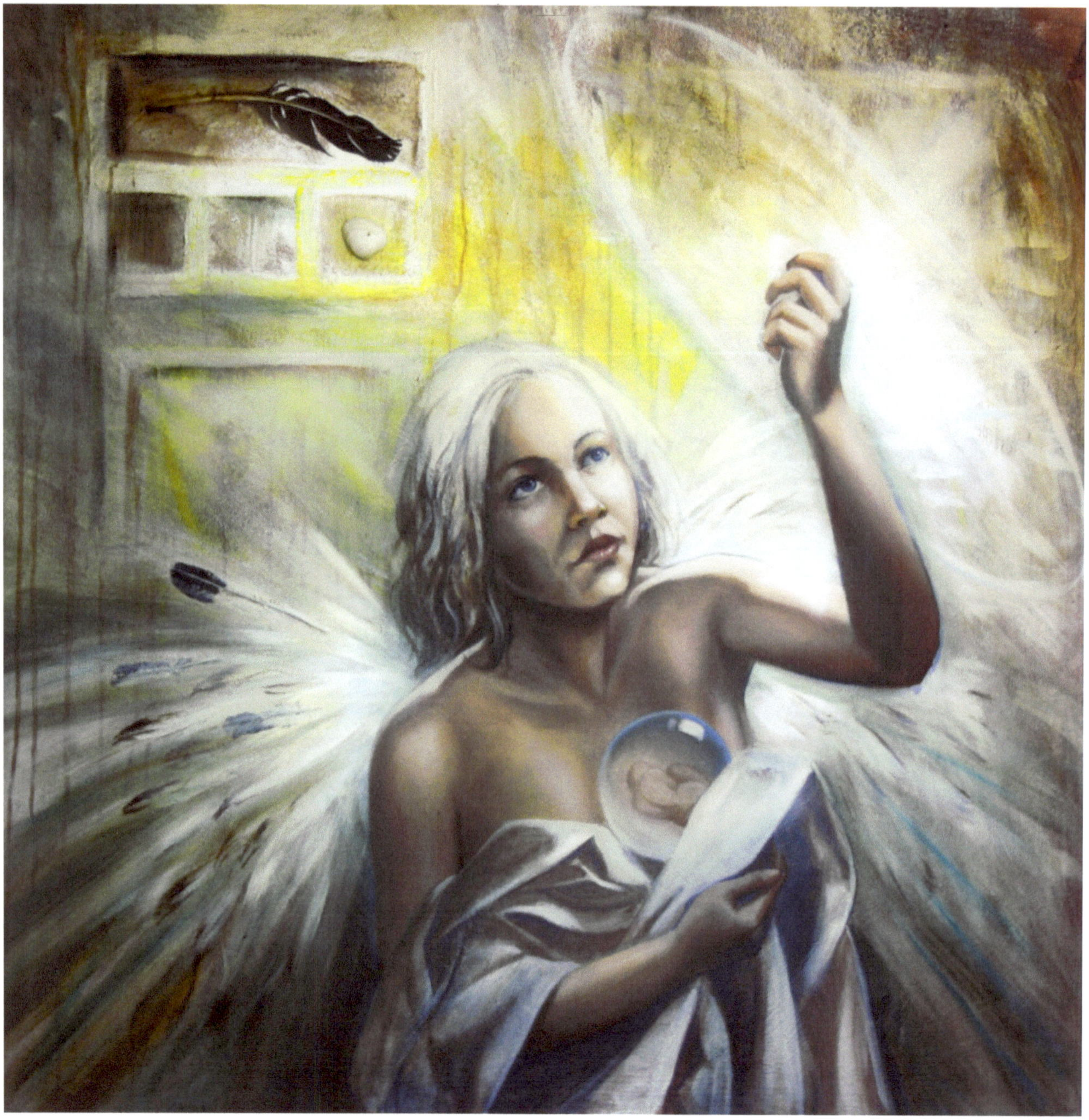

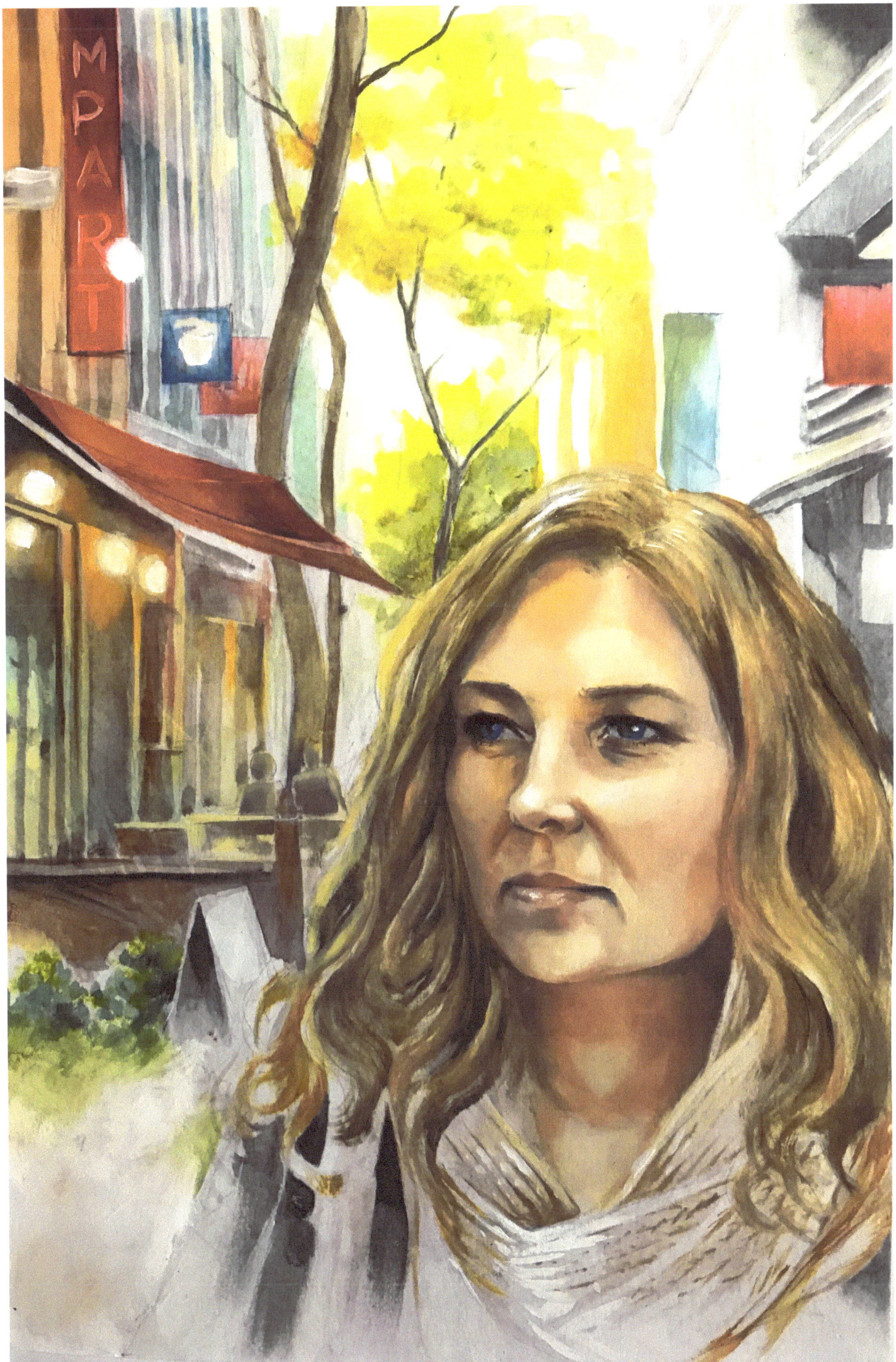
MPART

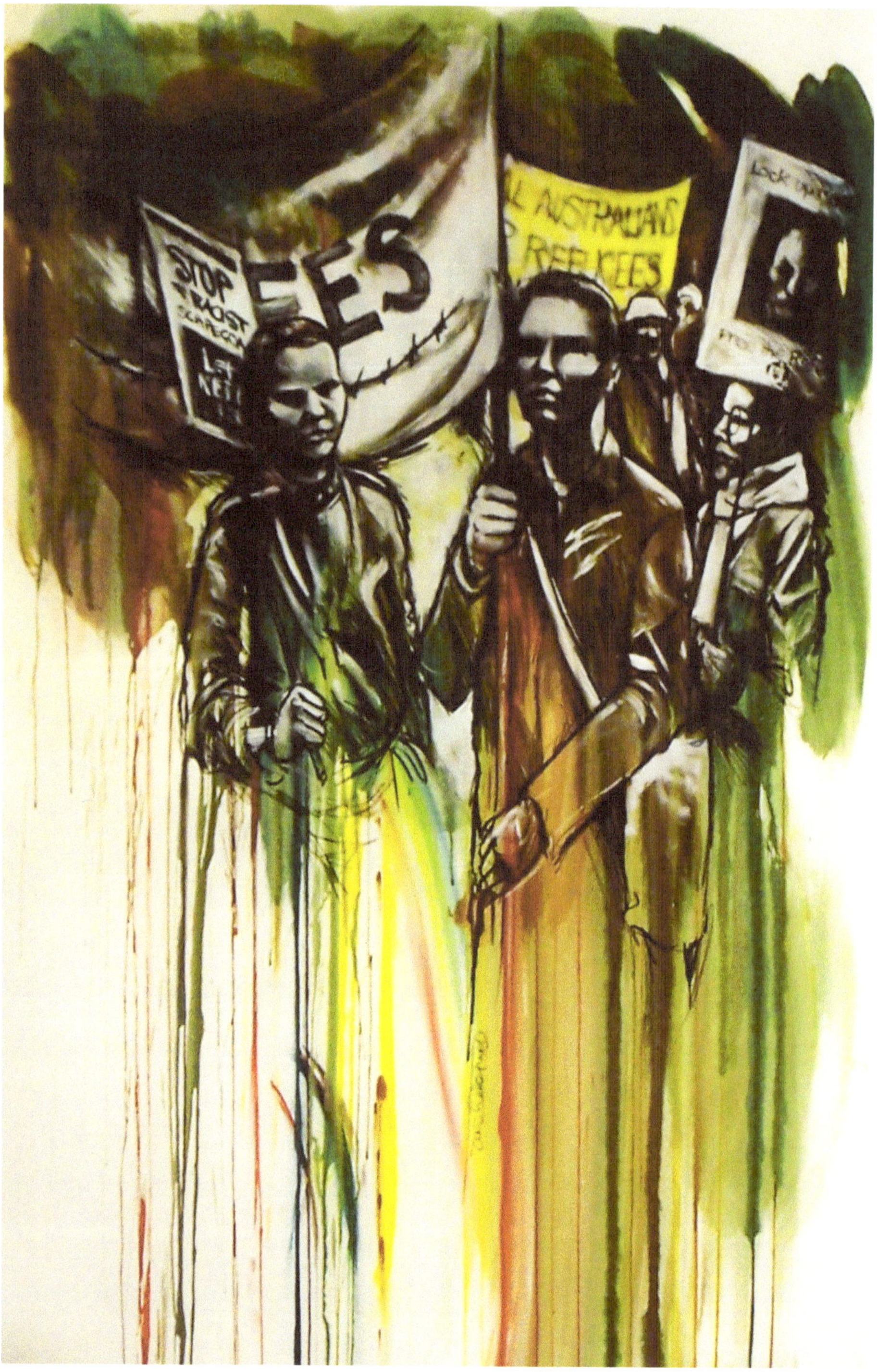
STOP
EES
AUSTRALIANS

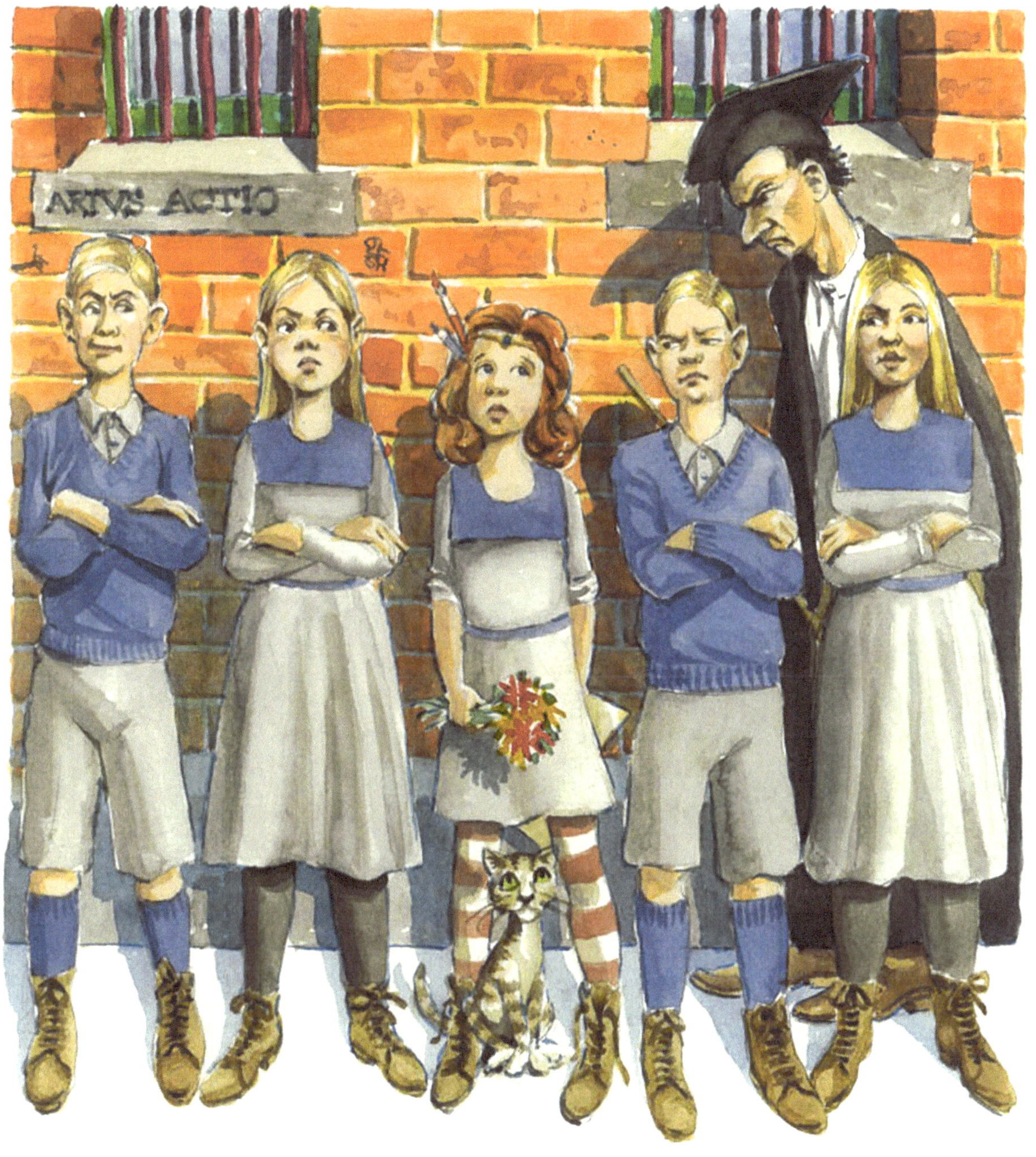
ARTVS ACTIO

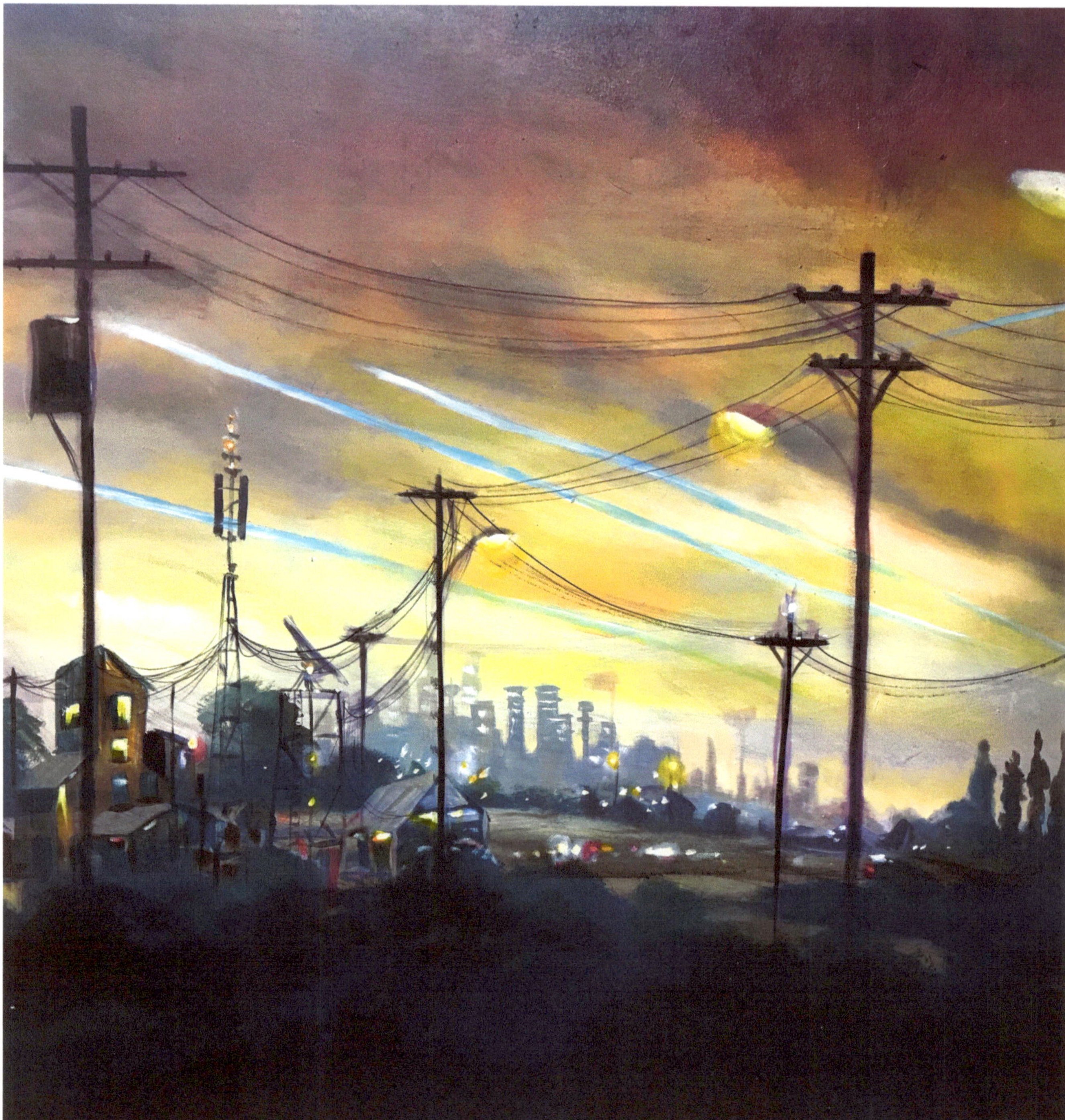

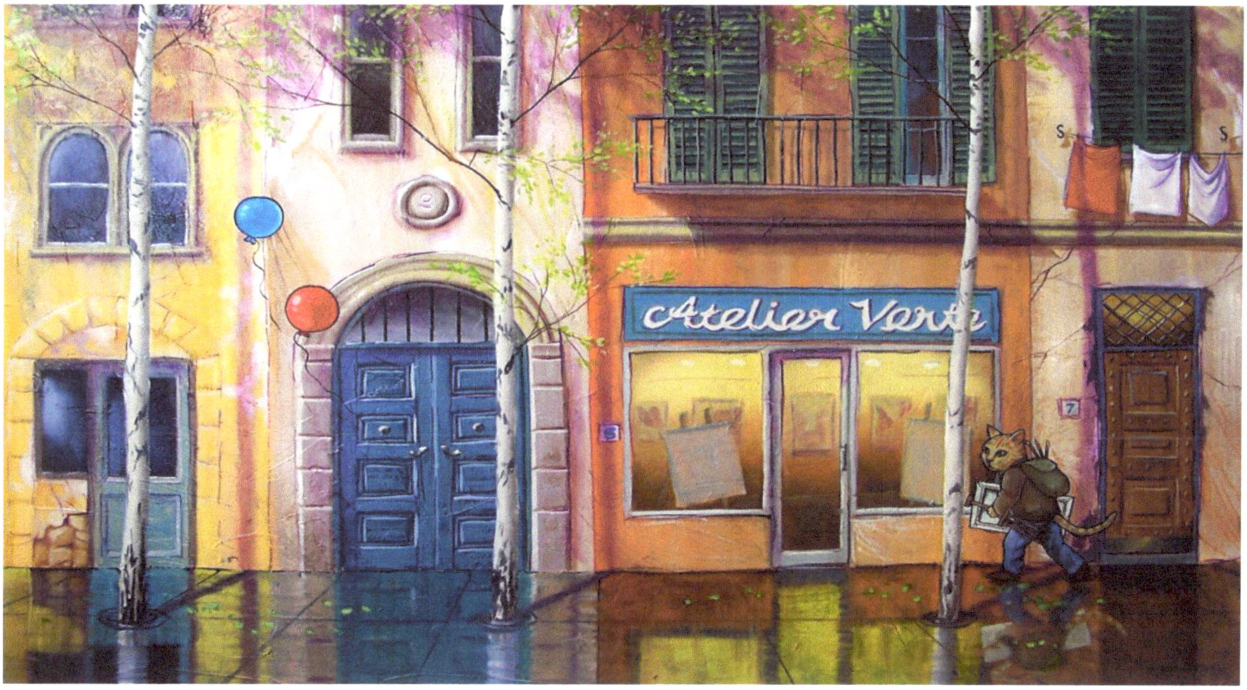
Atelier Vert

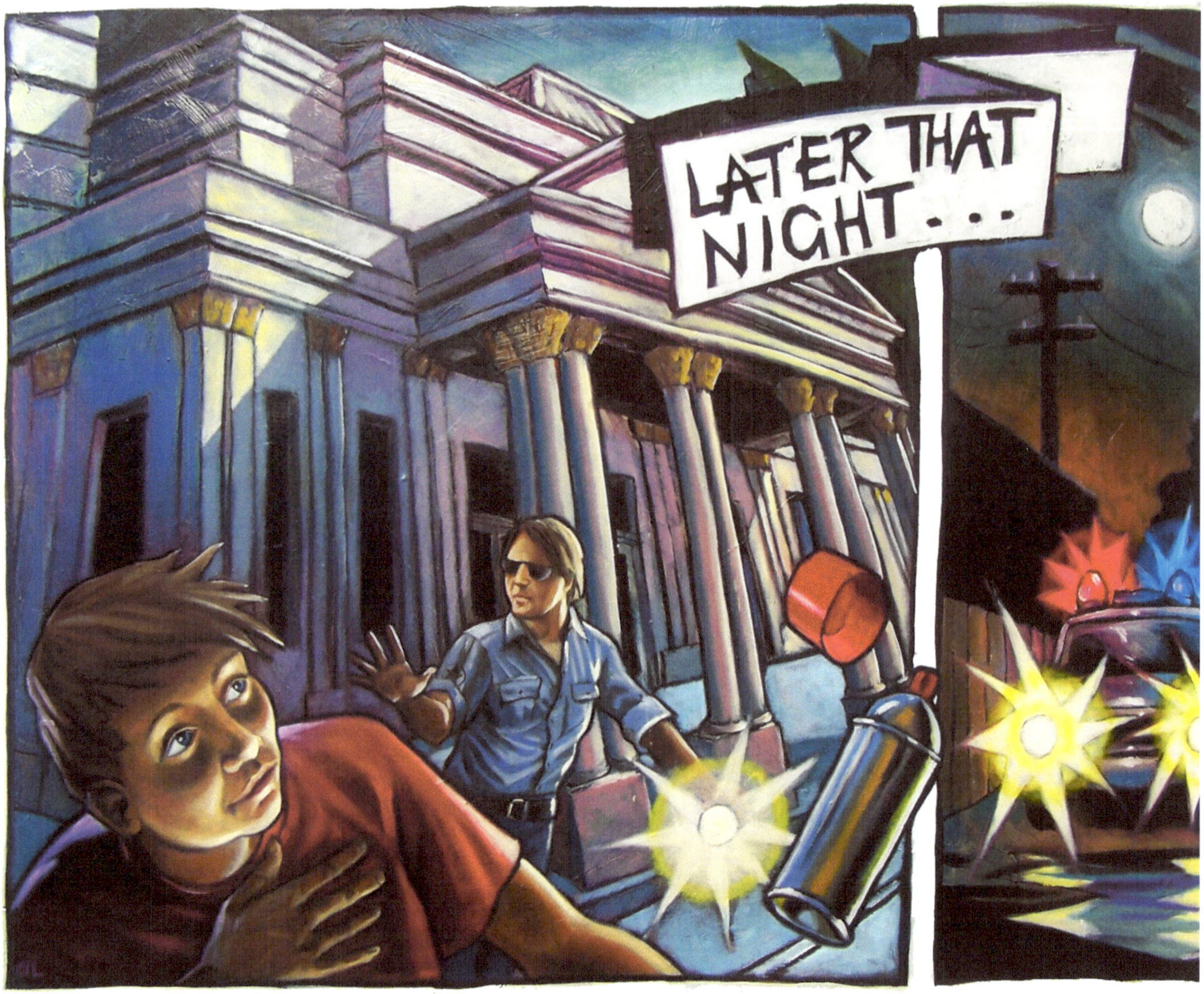
LATER THAT NIGHT...

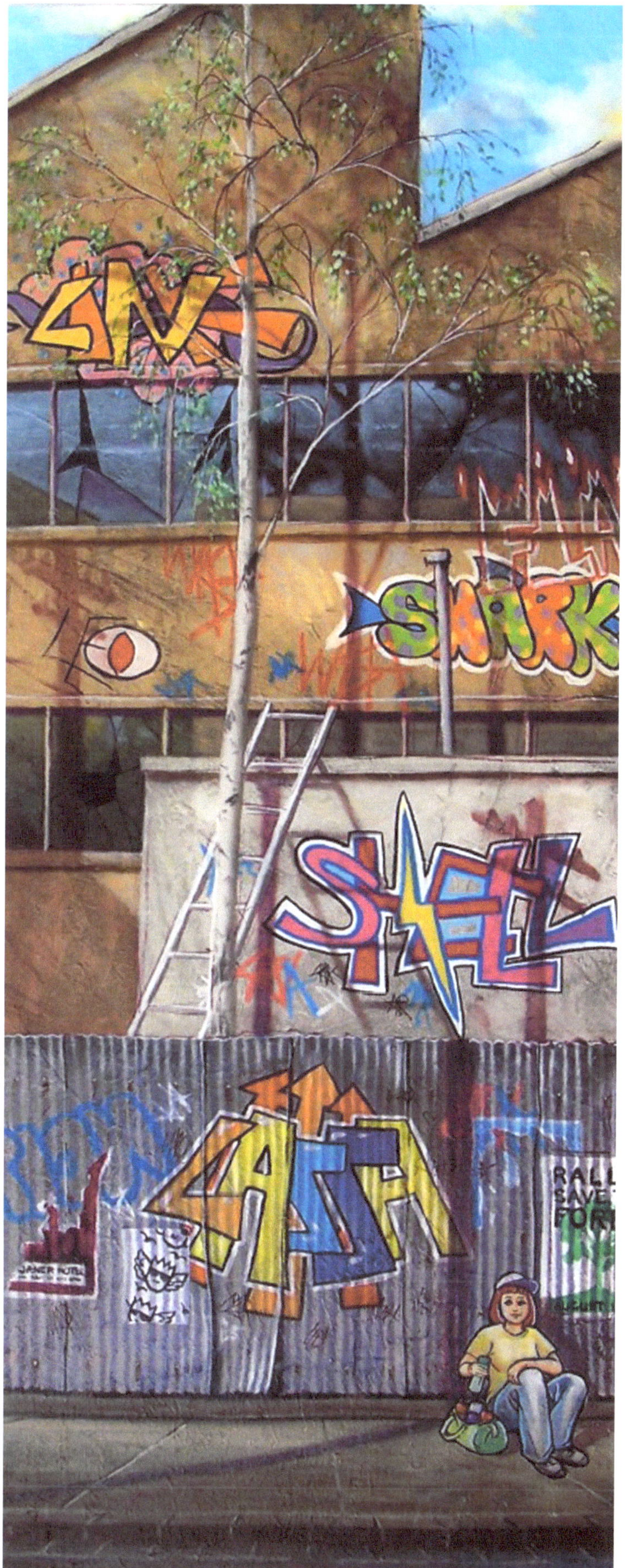

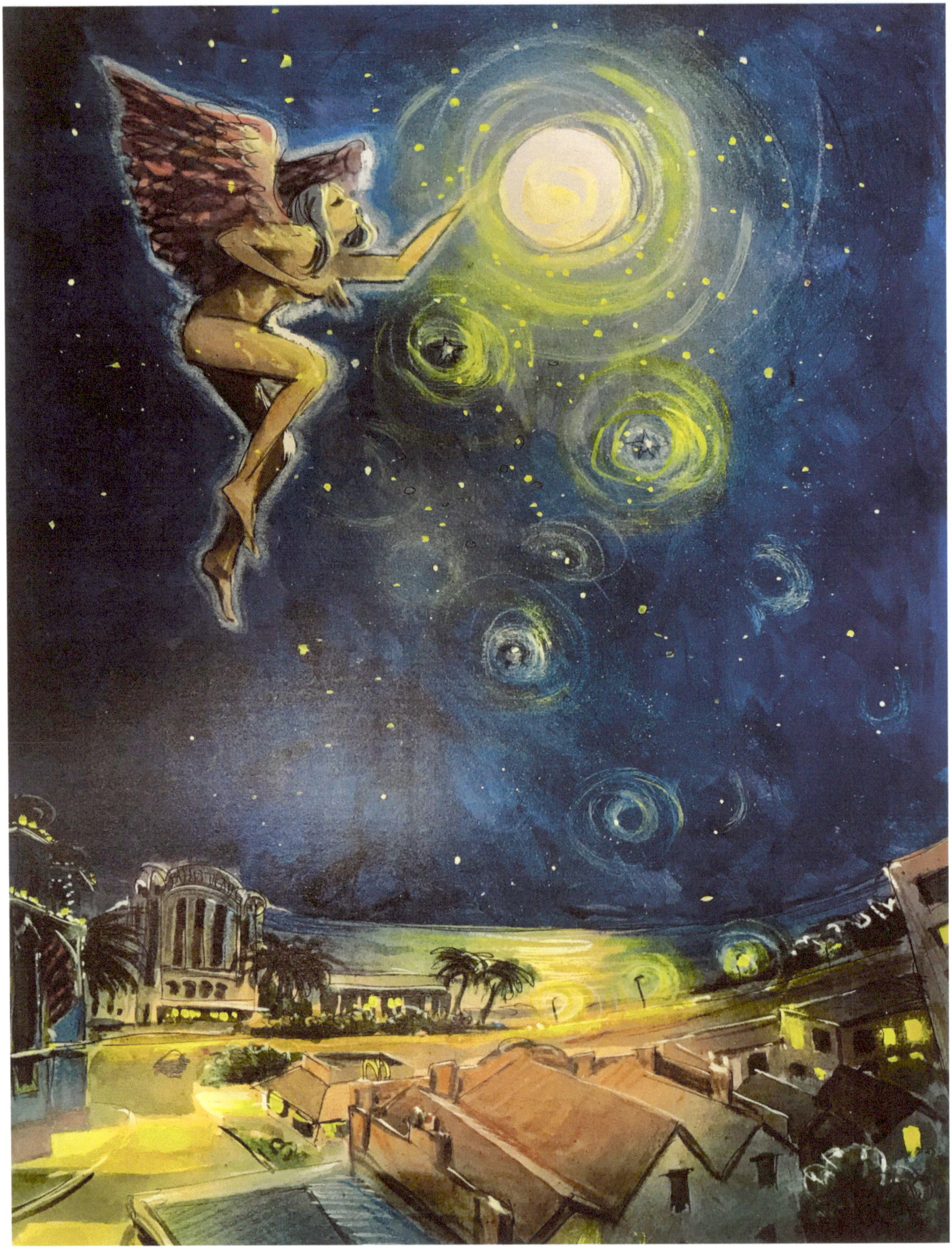

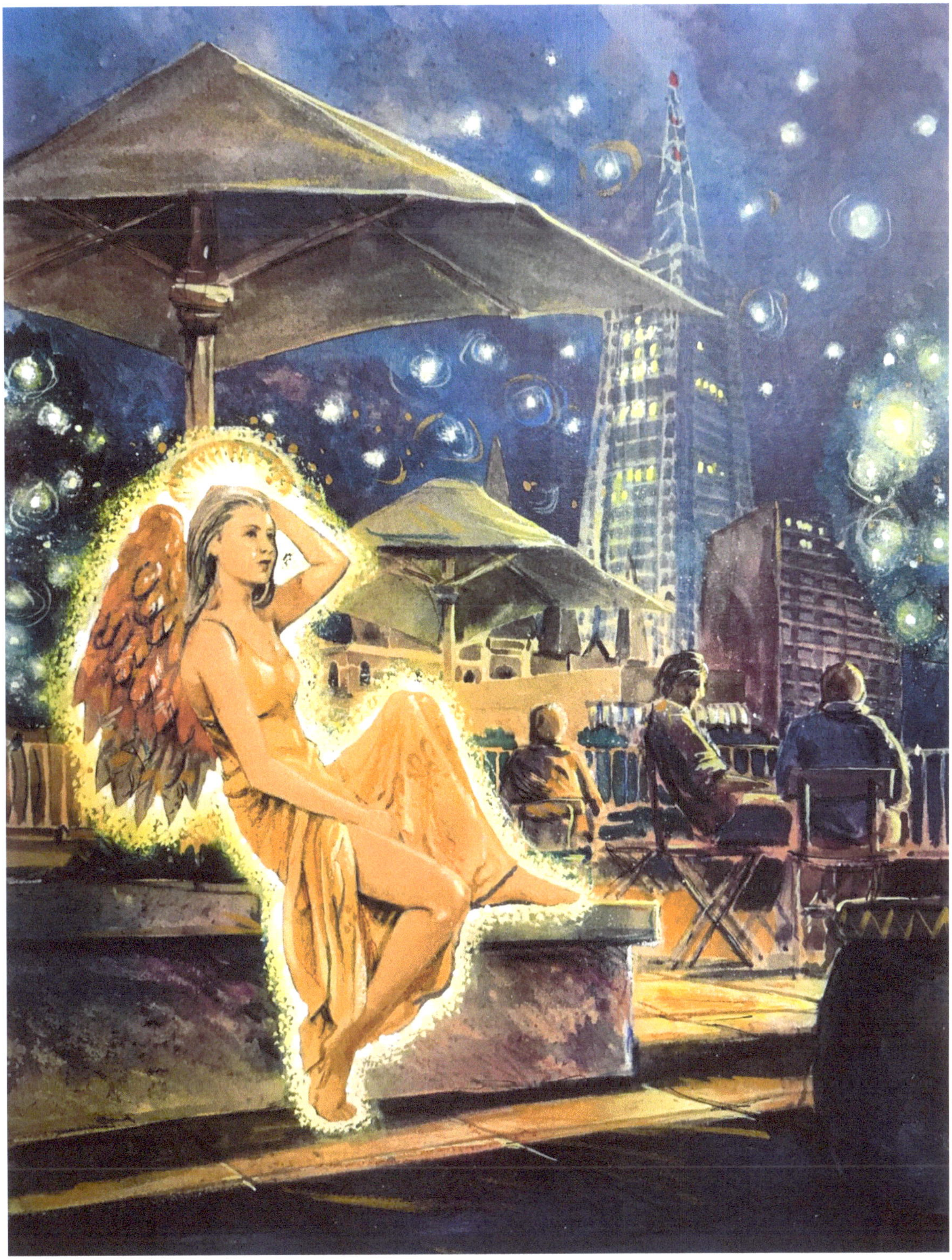

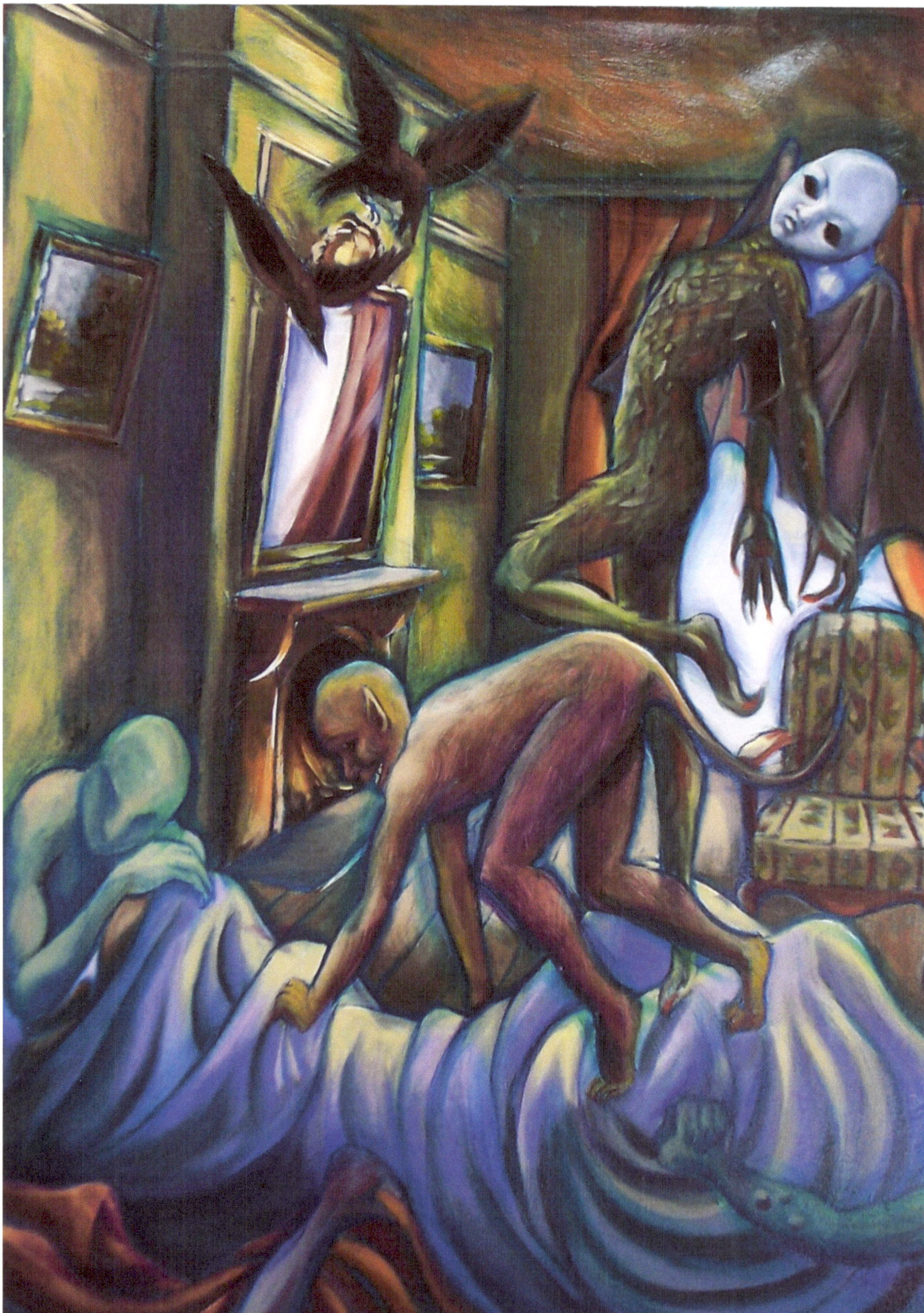

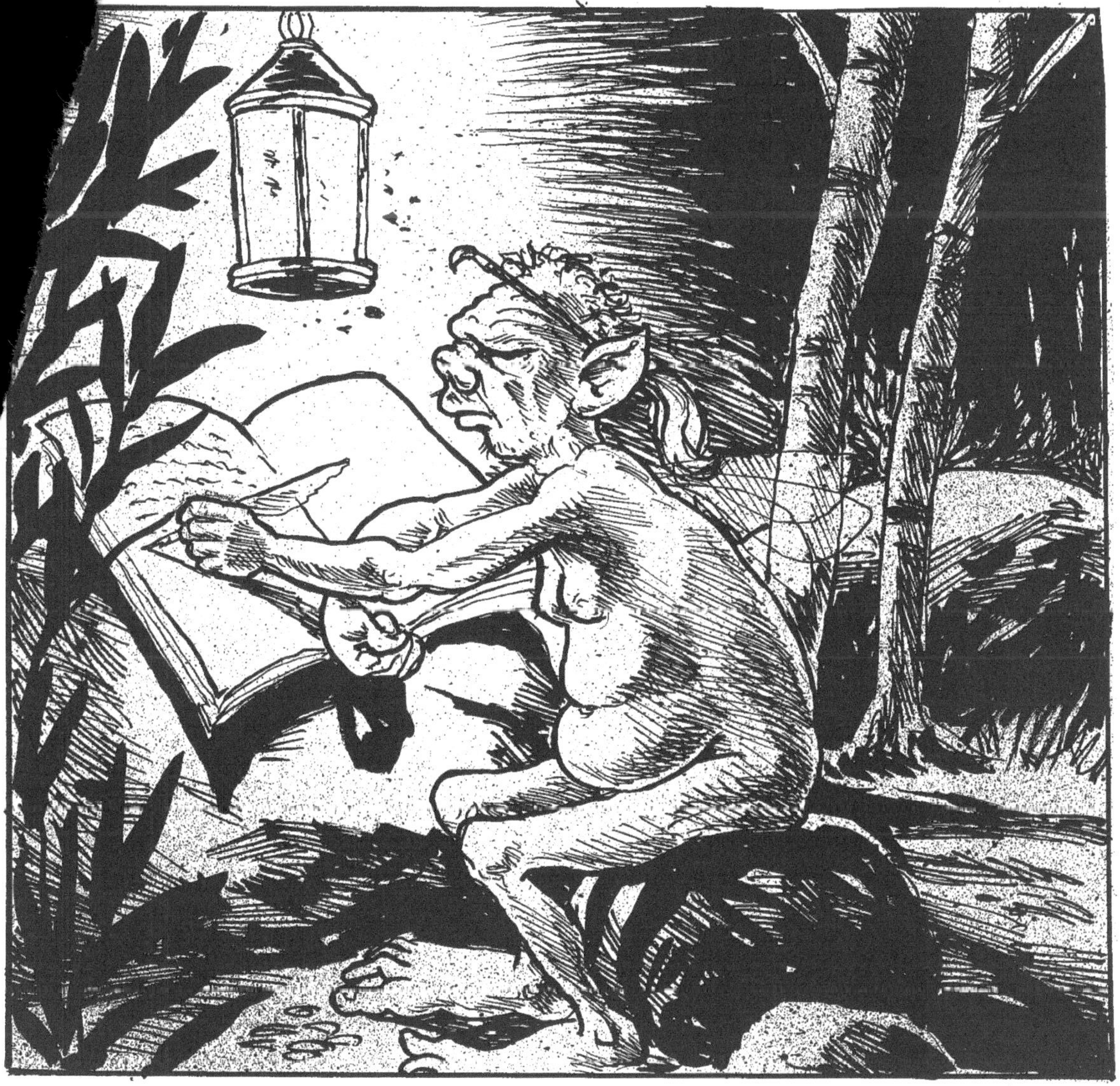

John Lawry - born Wodonga, Australia 1955

website johnlawryart.com email johnlawryart123@gmail.com

www.ingramcontent.com/pod-product-compliance
Ingram Content Group UK Ltd.
Pitfield, Milton Keynes, MK11 3LW, UK
UKHW061032310726
14089UKWH00009B/202
* 9 7 8 0 6 4 8 1 7 1 0 5 8 *